Nadia Sawalha

GREEDY GIRL'S DIET

Second Helpings!

Nadia Sawalha

GREEDY GIRL'S DIET

Second Helpings!

Fab food fast for a slim life

Photography by Nicky Johnston and Gavin Kingcome

KYLE BOOKS

This book is dedicated to all you amazing
Greedy Girls out there – tuck in!
All my love, Nadia xx

First published in Great Britain in 2014 by
Kyle Books, an imprint of Kyle Cathie Ltd
67–69 Whitfield Street
London W1T 4HF
general.enquiries@kylebooks.com
www.kylebooks.com

10 9 8 7 6 5 4 3 2 1

ISBN 978 0 85783 215 3

Text © 2014 Nadia Sawalha
Design © 2014 Kyle Books
Author photography © 2014 Nicky Johnston
Food photography © 2014 Gavin Kingcome*

*Except pages 54, 67, 93, 136, 144 and 157 © Doghouse
Media; pages 10–11, 46–47, 86–87, 120–121 and
178–179 © Will Heap; 152–153 © Lisa Linder; 4–5 ©
Keiko Oikawa; 129 © Charlie Richards; 122–123 ©
Getty/Tim Robberts; 132–133 © Yuki Sugiura

Nadia Sawalha is hereby identified as
the author of this work in accordance with Section 77
of the Copyright, Designs and Patents Act 1988.

Editor: Kyle Cathie
Editorial Assistant: Tara O'Sullivan
Proofreader: Stephanie Evans
Designer: Dale Walker
Author Photographer: Nicky Johnston
Food Photographer: Gavin Kingcome
Food Stylists: Mima Sinclair and Rachel Wood
Prop Stylist: Krissy Tosi
Production: Lisa Pinnell

A Cataloguing in Publication record for this title is
available from the British Library.

Colour reproduction by ALTA London
Printed and bound in Italy by Printer Trento

The nutritional information given with each recipe is given
per serving. The salt content for does not include seasoning
salt as the amount you add is discretionary. Serving
suggestions are not included in the analyses.

CONTENTS

INTRODUCTION

Fellow Greedy Girls of the world, unite! I'm back again, with another brilliant (yes, it's all gone to my head – and not my waist, thank God) recipe book!

I am beyond excited to be bringing you so many super-greedy recipes. However, this time there's a bit of a twist, because (drum roll!) this time they're not only going to be utterly delicious, they're also going to be super-speedy to make!!

So, basically what I'm proposing is more food... even faster. What could be better?! Because, let's face it girls, although we all love our food and sometimes want nothing more than to spend hours in the kitchen cooking, mostly we want our food (and lots of it) on the table, about as quickly as we can possibly get it there!

Whether we've had a day slogging it out at the office or indeed slogging it out with the kids (little darlings that they are!), the last thing we want to do is lose any sofa-and-wine time! Which is precisely why I've spent the last few months creating over a hundred delectable recipes for us to ensure that once we are on that sofa (as soon as humanly possible) with our feet up – we can stay there!

But, we don't want to be cooking just for ourselves, do we? No. We want to cook meals that we can eat with our friends and/or family rather than feeling like some social outcast eating our miserably defined 'diet food', in a corner like some freak. In fact, did you know that some women have been known to actually eat in the shed rather than with their family so as not to be tempted by what their family is eating! Erm... more than a little insane, don't you think?! As

they say, one definition of insanity is repeating the same behaviour again and again, always believing there will be a different outcome, and, as we all know (mostly from bitter experience), so much about dieting is insane.

In my 'fat girl to slim girl' opinion, denial is almost always the dark destroyer of any quest to shift body lard. Denial usually leads to The Big Binge, which of course leads to self loathing, which then, surprise, surprise, leads to... you've got it... another Big Binge. And so it goes on... and on... and on.

So throughout this scrumptious book I've laughed in the face of denial and packed it full of all the foods we love! Steaming hot bowls of pasta, gorgeous gooey cakes, satisfyingly spicy curries, monumental mountains of chips, super sexy stir fries, Sunday roast banquets – and did I say that lovely word... cake? Oh yes, I did. So good, I've said it twice! In fact, let's say it again: CAKE! I've even come up with a slimmer girl cocktail.

Throughout the book you will find the perfect recipe for whatever your speedy food desire is. If it's raging PMT that only something super-sweet and speedy will fix, I have the answer. If it's a hangover from hell that threatens all resolve to be slim, happy and healthy, I have the answer. If you need to get into that little black dress, like, YESTERDAY, well, I even have the answer to that too! I told you I was good, didn't I?

So come on, you lovely lot. Turn the page and enter a world of guilt-free foody heaven. I promise you won't be disappointed because, with every recipe I've created, I've stayed true to the mantra 'Greedy girls like it fast and they like it tasty.'

10 MINUTES AND UNDER

Delicious, super speedy dishes

MEALS IN UNDER 10 MINUTES... YES, 10 MINUTES!

Have you ever had one of those days when you find yourself expending most of your energy ducking-and-diving to avoid all those temptingly evil calorie-laden landmines of edible debauchery, only to walk straight through your front door and, within a matter of seconds, find you've morphed into a depraved 'Monster Muncher', raiding the contents of your fridge, cupboards and, on a bad day, even the backs of your drawers?

Now, you may not be familiar with the term 'Monster Muncher', but I am willing to bet the contents of my fridge (especially given the fact that you're currently holding a book with the word 'diet' in the title) that you have a good idea of what it must mean.

The 'Monster Muncher' is a particularly evil little beast that will often (rather cruelly, I think) manifest itself after a day of 'excellent' (groan!) eating behaviour.

Also known as the Grub Gremlin, it's that thing that clambers onto your shoulder at exactly the point you've 'done well' or 'made some progress' on the eating front. The villainous voice that whispers into your ear, 'Go on, just one bite won't do any harm. You deserve it. You've worked so hard. Go on... Reward yourself.'

The Monster Muncher is a particularly evil little beast that will often (rather cruelly, I think) manifest itself after a day of excellent eating behaviour.

You must know the kind of day I mean – it's always the same kind of day when he (and believe me, I am certain it is a he!) arrives. It's the kind of day when it feels as though the entire world has been trying to con you into thinking that everything would be made *soooo* much better if you simply take that first bite of something naughty. And the Monster Muncher digs its claws in tighter and tighter the more successfully you manage to say 'No' throughout the day.

You grapple with it, but manage to exclaim 'No' to the frothy coffee and Danish at the café en route to work! You manage a resistant but definitely audible 'Yes' to the muesli and yogurt perched on the top shelf of the fridge in the staff room instead!

You close down all discussion with a quick-fire 'No, I couldn't!' when a lunch of burger and chips with your colleagues rears its ugly head, instead managing to feel superior as you prepare your mackerel salad!

You turn your back firmly and resolutely on those come-hither vending machines that seem to be breeding and multiplying in virtually every public place! You manage to laugh in the face of those dirty, flirty hot dog stands, that pastry shop, those news kiosks with meticulously lined up sweets, chocolate bars and flapjacks. In the face of dieting adversity, you've almost achieved a smug day of dieting success! Hooray! You're journeying home, smiling with a sense of pride and achievement, knowing that you've managed to abandon a pound or half a pound of excess weight somewhere in your day.

Hooray! Wave the flags, put up the

bunting, and fire the guns!

UNTIL... your key goes into the front door. There's a groan from your tummy. Somehow, your eyes adopt a blank expression and you suddenly resemble a starving zombie. You pad through the front door, ignoring the various hellos from partner, child or pet. A homing beacon seems to have locked you into an inevitable path towards the kitchen. You're dazed and confused. You're no longer the victor, the superhero who has accomplished so much. No – you're becoming the victim. The put-upon. You are fast becoming the person who has made too many sacrifices today! You're starving. More starving than you've ever been in your life. Today is different. Today your hunger is more extreme than any other day. And BANG! He has landed: the Monster Muncher, the Grub Gremlin – whatever you want to call him, he is sitting on your shoulder and he is excitedly pointing out all the dangerous options on offer before you!

Stupidly, you entertain the thought that because you're home, you're somehow safe. You can fight this urge.

You can ignore the gremlin's temptations. You might even block his advances for a second or two by biting the end off a carrot or crunching excessively and eagerly on a celery stick. But then, all of a sudden, the Monster Muncher lurking deep inside you growls a little louder and, before you know it, he is unleashed!

You rapidly become a frenzy of gnashing teeth and snapping jaws. You become someone you hope no one close to you ever sees or witnesses. Your head darts left and right in a mania of monster munching as you grab, open and devour anything and everything before you!!

Within seconds, there's a hunk of cheese lodged in your throat, rapidly followed by an enormous swig of wine to wash it down, before you blindly ram a bundle of salami into your gob! They say sharks close their eyes just before they go in for the kill so they don't see the damage they're about to inflict. You are now like a Great White in your very own kitchen, with your prey all neatly arranged on every shelf of your fridge!

There's a moment when you pause – a flicker of sanity. Your eyes open. 'Is this reversible?' you think. 'Can I stop this?'

You answer in the only way you know (don't forget the Monster Muncher is still at large), and you scoop an enormous spoonful of peanut butter onto your tongue. The scene is barbaric. It's ugly.

You pause, panting, and then he's off again! The Monster growls, the Gremlin does his deed. A slug of custard will do it! You may have won the battles of the dieting day, but the war has definitely now been lost... ALL LOST!

Well – my fellow Jekyll and Hyders, all is not yet lost! Not quite! Yes – with a little help from yours truly... there is indeed another way. The recipes that I've laid out here will help you kick that Monster Muncher to the kerb. But do beware! However successfully you manage to rid yourself of the Monster Muncher inside, he will always be lurking just outside whatever room you find yourself eating in. Rest assured, he will be out there, waiting and hoping you'll slip and fall. Stick to my suggestions – and you can keep him flaming well out there!

The recipes that I've laid out here will help you kick that Monster Muncher to the kerb.

385 CALS / **21g** FAT / **5.3g** SAT FAT / **0.7g** SUGARS / **6.77g** SALT

EGG ROLLS

How funky are these little babies? I sometimes make piles of them when I have parties and they always go down a storm.

SERVES 4

For the egg rolls
½ tablespoon vegetable oil
6 spring onions, finely chopped
8 large eggs

For the filling
500g smoked salmon, smoked
  chicken or ham
4 handfuls rocket
soy sauce, for drizzling

Heat the oil in a large, non-stick frying pan over a medium heat. Throw in the spring onions and cook for a couple of minutes. Then take your onions out with a slotted spoon, set aside, and reduce the heat a little.

Whisk the eggs lightly in a jug or bowl and add the spring onions to them. Now pour a quarter of the egg mixture into the pan and swirl it about until it evenly coats the base. Cook until it's set and then slide it onto a plate. Repeat three times, keeping your cooked egg pancakes warm as you go.

Now divide your smoked salmon, chicken or ham and rocket equally between the egg pancakes, drizzle with a little soy sauce, then roll and serve.

Those of you who like a little fire might want to swap the soy sauce for Tabasco. And for a veggie version, substitute the salmon, chicken or ham for some lightly fried mushrooms.

234 CALS / **12g** FAT / **2.4g** SAT FAT / **2.7g** SUGARS / **0.96g** SALT

SPICY MIDDLE EASTERN BEANS

*This a hugely popular breakfast all over the Middle East. I love it, but not for breakfast –
it's a bit too dramatic for early in the morning! But I love it any other time of the day! It's
one of my Dad's favourite dishes. He adds a little chopped fresh green chilli on top, so if you
like things hot, why not do the same?*

SERVES 4

400g tin fava beans
2 tablespoons tahini
juice of ½ lemon
½ garlic clove, finely chopped
   or crushed
good pinch of salt

For the topping
4 hard-boiled eggs, quartered
sprinkle of cayenne pepper
chopped fresh flat-leaf parsley or
   fresh coriander

Place a small saucepan over a medium heat. Add the
beans and their liquid and heat until warmed through.

Put the tahini into a small bowl and then mix in the
lemon juice, garlic and salt. It will go all sticky and yucky,
but don't worry, because as you now add 2 tablespoons
warm water the consistency will change to a nice,
smooth, creamy one. If (ahhh!) it doesn't, just add a bit
more water.

Now gently mash the heated beans in a wide bowl (don't
drain the liquid), leaving some of them whole. Drizzle the
tahini mixture on top.

Garnish with the eggs, cayenne pepper and chopped
herbs. Serve with one warmed wholemeal pitta each.

45 | **10** | **15**
MINUTES
30

320 CALS / **13.9g** FAT / **4.8g** SAT FAT / **6.7g** SUGARS / **2.3g** SALT

CURRIED BAKED BEANS AND FRANKS

Students across the globe will love me for this recipe: it's cheap, easy-peasy and tastes like junk food whilst not actually being junk food!

SERVES 4

1 teaspoon oil
1 garlic clove (optional)
2 teaspoons curry powder
2 x 420g tins reduced-sugar baked
  beans
8 chicken frankfurters

Heat the oil in a non-stick saucepan and fry the garlic until softened – if you burn it, chuck it!

Stir in the curry powder and, once the aroma wafts from it, pour in the baked beans. Whilst they are heating, thinly slice the frankfurters and then chuck them in with the beans to heat them through. Bob's your uncle, Fanny's your aunt, it's ready to serve.

QUICK TIPS

For a veggie alternative, why not replace the chicken frankfurters with mushrooms or even vegetarian sausages?

361 CALS / **7g** FAT / **2.1g** SAT FAT / **3.5g** SUGARS / **0.18g** SALT

RED BASGHETTI
(NAMED BY MY DAUGHTERS)

This is my daughters' favourite meal 'ever ever in the whole wide world', which is rather handy as it's so quick to get on the table! They, of course, will not tolerate the 'smelly' Parmesan cheese suggested here, so when I make it for them I swap it for Cheddar or sometimes stir in a tablespoon of low-fat cream cheese instead.

SERVES 4

350g spaghetti
1 tablespoon olive oil
1 juicy garlic clove
1 tablespoon tomato purée
handful of basil (optional)
4 tablespoons freshly grated
  Parmesan cheese
salt

Cook your spaghetti according to the packet instructions (I hate it when recipe books say that, but sorry, it's the right thing to say!), making sure, as the Italian mamas say, that the water is as salty as the sea (there you go, something extra).

Meanwhile, heat the oil gently in a large, heavy-based frying pan over a medium heat. Add the garlic and cook until softened but not browned (if you burn it, chuck it – it will ruin the whole dish). Then add your tomato purée and fry a little, stirring the whole time. Then add a couple of tablespoons of water from the pasta pan (the starch in the water makes a difference) and stir to loosen the purée, adding a little more water if you think it needs it.

Drain your pasta, plop it into the frying pan and toss it in your tomato-garlicky yumminess. Add the basil (if using), divide between four bowls and sprinkle a tablespoon of Parmesan over each.

Serve with salad.

280 CALS / **12g** FAT / **2.2g** SAT FAT / **3.9g** SUGARS / **0.82g** SALT

PRAWN AND AVOCADO JUMBLE

I know using the word 'jumble' in a recipe title is very cheffy and show-offy but when you see the finished dish, you will see why I have used it... I hope, otherwise you will think I am cheffy and show-offy!

SERVES 4

1 tablespoon olive oil
1 garlic clove, finely chopped
1 red chilli, finely chopped
600g raw, peeled prawns
½ green pepper, finely chopped
handful of finely chopped fresh
  flat-leaf parsley
1 ½ small avocados, cubed
2 x 198g tins no added sugar
  sweetcorn, drained

Heat the oil in a frying pan over a medium heat. Add the garlic and chilli and soften, then throw in your prawns and stir them until they turn, as if by magic, to the prettiest shade of pink.

Take your pan off the heat (and you won't believe it girls, we're nearly ready to eat), stir in the rest of the ingredients and serve.

QUICK TIPS

Avocado has got to be one of my favourite foods – it's full of good fats (yes, they exist!) and vitamins, and one avocado contains more potassium than a banana.

186 CALS / **8g** FAT / **1g** SAT FAT / **8.4g** SUGARS / **1.17g** SALT

QUINOA TABBOULEH SALAD

Superfood is a word bandied about a lot these days (and used as a great marketing term for many products) but I believe quinoa (pronounced keen-wa) truly is a superfood. It manages to be a carbohydrate as well as a protein (impressive, huh?), is soooo easy to cook and has a gorgeous, slightly nutty, taste. I use it all the time and keep a bowl of it in the fridge so I can add it to soups and salads whenever I want. I even have it for breakfast sometimes with yogurt and fresh fruit!

SERVES 4

200g quinoa
½ chicken or veg stock cube
50g fresh flat-leaf parsley,
   chopped
handful of fresh mint, chopped
3 sticks of celery, finely chopped
½ green pepper, finely chopped
2 carrots, finely chopped
8 small tomatoes, finely diced

For the dressing
1 garlic clove
2 tablespoons olive oil
juice of ½ lemon
½ shallot, finely chopped
salt

To serve
2 tablespoons dry-fried pine nuts
   or walnuts

Put the quinoa in a non-stick pan with ½ chicken or veg stock cube and pour boiling water over it to about 5cm above the quinoa. Simmer for about 10 minutes until the water is absorbed and the grains have started to unfurl and then allow to cool. (If you are in a hurry, just spread it out on a plate and it will cool down really quickly.)

Meanwhile, make the dressing. Put the garlic clove on a fork, then put the rest of the dressing ingredients in a small bowl and whisk with the fork. Put to one side with the garlic fork left resting in the dressing to infuse it with garlic loveliness without making it too strong.

When you are ready to eat, put the quinoa, fresh herbs, celery, green pepper, carrots and tomatoes into a bowl, then stir in the dressing, scatter over the nuts and *voilà!* It's ready.

Grilled lean lamb chops would work nicely with this – but in that case, omit the nuts.

237 CALS / **9g** FAT / **2.1g** SAT FAT / **6.8g** SUGARS / **0.55g** SALT

GUACAMOLE AND PITTA CHIPS

Oh boy, who on earth doesn't love guacamole? A gift from the gods, as far as I'm concerned, but also very fattening if not eaten with a little caution, which of course is very hard to do! So I have swapped some of the avocado with petits pois to reduce the calories a bit without reducing any of the taste or health benefits! Why not add some crudités to this for a bit of extra filling power?

SERVES 4

280g frozen petits pois
1½ small ripe avocados, roughly
   chopped
small bunch of fresh coriander,
   finely chopped
1 green pepper, finely diced
1 gorgeously red but firm tomato,
   finely diced
¼ red onion, very finely diced
zest and juice of 1 lime

For the pitta chips
3 wholemeal pitta breads
olive oil spray
sea salt

First make the pitta chips. Preheat the oven to 200°C/ Gas 5. Slice the pitta breads in half horizontally so they separate into two thin pieces. Then, using a pair of scissors, cut them into tortilla chip-sized triangles. Lay them out onto a baking tray and, using your oil sprayer, lightly spray them. Then sprinkle them with sea salt and pop them into the oven for 8–10 minutes.

To make the guacamole, pour boiling water over the petits pois. Leave for a minute and then drain. Then put them in a blender with the avocados and pulse a few times until the mixture has a coarse consistency. Put into a bowl, stir in the rest of the ingredients and serve the guacamole with the pitta chips.

382 CALS / 9.5g FAT / 3g SAT FAT / 8.8g SUGARS / 3.32g SALT

QUESADILLAS

I love these not-so-naughty but nice quesadillas and usually have them on a Saturday night whilst watching a movie with the family! If you want to make them a bit naughtier, add some low-fat crème fraîche to replace the traditional (very fattening) sour cream.

SERVES 4

½ tablespoon oil
1 onion, finely chopped
2 garlic cloves, finely chopped
1 teaspoon ground cumin
400g tin pinto or kidney beans, drained
8 flour tortillas
100g low-fat Cheddar cheese, grated
4 fresh tomatoes, chopped
2 tablespoons chopped fresh coriander
salt and freshly ground black pepper

Pour the oil into a large frying pan and fry the onion, garlic and cumin until the onion and garlic are soft. Pour in the beans and 1 tablespoon water. Warm the beans through, mashing them with a fork at the same time to break them up a bit. Season very well.

Now divide the beans between 4 of the tortillas and scatter the cheese, tomatoes and coriander on top. Top each with another tortilla.

Wipe out the frying pan and reheat it. Cook each quesadilla for 1–2 minutes on each side until golden.

QUICK TIPS

Although, as I said, I love eating these on movie night, it's best to leave yourself a good few hours between your last meal of the day and bed time in order to give your body time to burn it off – in time for breakfast next day!

121 CALS / **4g** FAT / 0.6g SAT FAT / **1.9g** SUGARS / **0.58g** SALT

SPICY PRAWNS WITH SPINACH AND CHERRY TOMATOES

You could serve this super spicy dish with my favourite wonder food, quinoa, or maybe some roast plantain. I think a winter slaw made of grated carrot, cabbage and a little onion would also work really well, not just because it's delicious, but also because it would mean MORE munching! #greedy

SERVES 4

1 tablespoon olive oil
250g tiny cherry tomatoes
3 garlic cloves, thinly sliced
1 red chilli, finely chopped
   (optional)
400g raw, peeled prawns
1 teaspoon jerk seasoning
large handful of spinach
salt and freshly ground black
   pepper

Heat the oil in a wok or heavy-based pan and fry the tomatoes until they blister. Let them cook for a minute or so and then throw in the garlic and chilli (if using). Cook, whilst stirring, for about 30 seconds.

Sprinkle the prawns evenly with the jerk spice, throw them into the pan and fry them until they turn pink. Then stir in your spinach until it just wilts. Season well.

Serve with salad or steamed veg.

220 CALS / **9g** FAT / **2.4g** SAT FAT / **0.4g** SUGARS / **2.52g** SALT

FRIED SMOKED SALMON AND POACHED EGGS

This makes a rather glamorous change to the more traditional egg and bacon muffin and, of course, it's far better for you, too! Maybe a small glass of champagne would go awfully well with it!

SERVES 4

1 teaspoon vinegar

4 large eggs

2 wholemeal muffins

6 slices of smoked salmon, cut into strips

2 handfuls of watercress

sea salt

Bring a saucepan of water up to the bubble. Add a good pinch of salt and the vinegar. Whisk the water quickly until it is swirling, then crack in your eggs one by one. Turn the heat off and leave them to poach for 4 minutes.

While the eggs are cooking, split and toast the muffins.

Meanwhile, place a heavy-based, non-stick frying pan over a medium heat and fry the smoked salmon in two batches until crisp.

Remove your poached eggs from the water with a slotted spoon and place them on a piece of kitchen paper to drain. Arrange your toasted muffins on four plates. Lay the watercress on top, then the poached eggs and finish off with the crispy smoked salmon.

If you're really hungry, treat yourself to a whole muffin, just like I have in this picture!

195 CALS / **6g** FAT / **1.3g** SAT FAT / **5g** SUGARS / **0.84g** SALT

PARISIAN PLAICE WITH A MOUTARDE* SAUCE

I am specific about the type of mustard used in this recipe because I think it makes a real difference* to the finished dish, but, of course, feel free to use whatever you fancy... bet you're nervous now, huh?!

SERVES 4

½ tablespoon olive oil

3 spring onions, finely chopped

4 large plaice or sole fillets

150ml white wine

2 tablespoons Grey Poupon unseeded Dijon mustard

200g low-fat crème fraîche

Heat the oil gently in a large, non-stick frying pan. Gently fry the spring onions until softened, then remove from the pan and put to one side.

Put the fish in the pan and cook for about a minute on each side. Pour in the wine and let it reduce a little. Then stir in the mustard and crème fraîche. Bring it all up to a bit of a bubble, then reduce the heat and let it simmer for 3–4 minutes before serving with petits pois.

Voilà, très French fish!

*Say in a French accent

464 CALS / **19g** FAT / **7.5g** SAT FAT / **2.6g** SUGARS / **3.43g** SALT

GUILT-FREE CROQUE-MADAME

I know what you're thinking... 'How can you have a guilt-free croque-madame?' Well, just try this and see – I promise it is yum! I usually have this super sarnie with a tomato and basil salad on the side.

SERVES 1

2 thin slices smoked ham
30g reduced-fat Cheddar cheese
  (make sure it's a good one!)
2 slices sourdough bread
reduced-fat butter, for spreading
1 medium egg
handful of cherry tomatoes
5 or 6 fresh basil leaves

Heat a non-stick frying pan over a medium heat.

Put the ham and cheese between the bread slices, press down firmly, then spread the reduced-fat butter on the outside of the sandwich on both sides.

Put into the preheated pan and push down with a fish slice. Cook until golden on both sides.

Meanwhile, poach the egg (see page 30).

When the croque is ready, top with the egg and serve with the cherry tomatoes and basil.

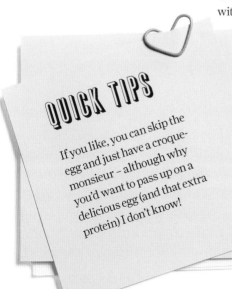

QUICK TIPS

If you like, you can skip the egg and just have a croque-monsieur – although why you'd want to pass up on a delicious egg (and that extra protein) I don't know!

309 CALS / **13g** FAT / **5.1g** SAT FAT / **2.9g** SUGARS / **3.09g** SALT

MEDITERRANEAN FLATBREAD PIZZA

This is one of my favourite Monster Muncher weapons because it feels so naughty and you can devour it really quickly. Now I know we plump birds are supposed to try and eat slooooowly, like the skinnies... but sometimes we just CAN'T!

SERVES 1

1 small wholemeal wrap
olive oil spray
1–2 teaspoons tomato purée
½ teaspoon dried oregano
50g (2 slices) ham
½ courgette, grated
4 black olives, pitted and halved
½ ball of low-fat mozzarella
sea salt and freshly ground
    black pepper

Put the grill on to a medium heat to warm up. Heat a non-stick frying pan with a heatproof handle over a medium heat.

Spray both sides of the wrap with olive oil and then spread the tomato purée on one side. Put the wrap, purée side up, in the frying pan. Layer the rest of the ingredients on top. Add some black pepper and a little salt then, after 2–3 minutes, put under the grill until the cheese is melty.

Pizza anyone?

I love pizza, but not the full, bloated feeling you sometimes get when you've overindulged on a heavy, doughy base. So swap the base for a wrap and enjoy all those delicious toppings with none of the guilt.

GREEK TOASTIE

I love lountza ham, but you can use any smoked ham you like – just make sure you remove any visible fat... groan! You will need a sandwich toaster for this recipe.

SERVES 1

2 slices seeded brown loaf
olive oil spray
1 slice lountza ham, or other
   smoked ham, fat removed
1 medium tomato, sliced
30g low-fat feta cheese, crumbled
good pinch dried oregano or a
   sprinkling of fresh
freshly ground black pepper

Spray one side of both bread slices with olive oil spray.

Place one slice of bread, oil-side down, into the sandwich toaster and then layer in the ham, tomato, feta and oregano.

Add a couple of grinds of black pepper, then place the other slice of bread on top, oily side up. Close the toaster and cook for 2–3 minutes until golden.

Serve with a large salad.

ITALIAN TOASTIE

Let's take a little trip to Italy...

SERVES 1

2 thin slices ciabatta
olive oil spray
1 teaspoon sundried tomato paste
2 slices Parma ham, fat removed
50g low-fat mozzarella
handful of rocket

Spray one side of both ciabatta slices with olive oil spray. Spread the tomato paste equally onto the dry sides. Put one slice, oil side down, into your sandwich toaster.

Lay on one slice Parma ham, followed by the mozzarella and the rocket, then top with the remaining slice of ham. Place the other slice of bread on top, oil side up. Close the toaster and cook for a couple of minutes before serving.

258 CALS / **6g** FAT / **2.5g** SAT FAT / **9.9g** SUGARS / **0.73g** SALT

DOUBLE CHEESE AND APPLE TOASTIE

Sometimes, if I have some in the fridge, I add a chopped mini gherkin or a couple of drained, chopped capers to this delicious sandwich.

SERVES 1

2 slices granary bread

olive oil spray

1 tablespoon low-fat cream cheese

1 tablespoon grated extra-mature
  low-fat Cheddar cheese

½ apple, grated

green part of 1 spring onion, finely
  chopped

Spray one side of both bread slices with the olive oil spray. Spread the other side of each with the cream cheese.

Put one slice of bread into the sandwich toaster, oil side down, and cream cheese side up. Top with the grated Cheddar, apple and spring onion. Lay the other slice of bread, oil side up, on top.

Close the toaster and cook for a couple of minutes, then serve.

Even if you're making a super-quick sandwich like the ones on this page, you should still give yourself time to sit down and eat properly. That way you'll appreciate it more, rather than being tempted to scoff another.

209 CALS / **6g** FAT / **3.7g** SAT FAT / **24.6g** SUGARS / **0.5g** SALT

BERRY ICED MOUSSE

This is a gorgeous, light dessert that you can whip up at a moment's notice.

SERVES 4

500g low-fat cream cheese
50g icing sugar
300g frozen berries mashed a
 little with a... well, a masher,
 I suppose!

Put the cream cheese and icing sugar into a bowl and, using an electric whisk, whisk until thoroughly combined and beautifully smooth.

Stir in the berries and, believe it or not, dessert is ready!

A WORD ABOUT DESSERTS

Those of you who are familiar with my food philosophy will know that I believe very strongly in enjoying a little of what you fancy. Desserts definitely fall into that category. It doesn't matter how healthy you are trying to be, there is always room for dessert. Just make the portion size a wee bit smaller, shave off a little of the sugar here, swap full-fat for low-fat there and, before you know it, you can whip up outrageously good puddings whilst still feeling completely saintly.

UNDER **10** MINUTES
45 / 0 / 15 / 30

45 CALS / **0g** FAT / **0g** SAT FAT / **9.8g** SUGARS / **0.01g** SALT

ROSY POSY RASPBERRIES

Ah, what a pretty summer's delight this dish is... You could turn this into a cocktail by adding a bottle of Prosecco to the bowl and sharing with five of your friends!

SERVES 4

400g fresh raspberries
2 tablespoons icing sugar
2 tablespoons rosewater
handful of fresh mint leaves

Put the raspberries in a pretty bowl.

Mix together the icing sugar and rosewater and drizzle over the raspberries. Decorate with the whole fresh mint leaves and serve.

This is a gorgeous, summery dish perfect for sharing with friends. Enjoying a beautiful dessert with great company is one of life's great pleasures – so leave your guilt behind and indulge.

UNDER 10 MINUTES 45 0 15 30

254 CALS / 1g FAT / 0.1g SAT FAT / 59.7g SUGARS / 0.03g SALT

WORKOUT FRUIT SALAD

I call this the Workout Fruit Salad because, as I grate, I'm working out my arms and doing my squats! How efficient!

SERVES 1

1 apple, halved and cored
1 nectarine, halved and stoned
1 pear, halved and cored
1 banana, sliced

Grate the apple, nectarine and pear into a bowl, then stir in the banana.

10 MINUTES 45 0 15 30

64 CALS / 0g FAT / 0.1g SAT FAT / 0.1g SUGARS / 0.02g SALT

MARSHMALLOW CRISPIE CAKES

SERVES 10

½ tablespoon low-fat spread
100g sugar-free mini marshmallows
100g puffed rice cereal

Line a 23cm square baking tray with baking paper. Melt the spread in a non-stick pan over a low heat, then add the marshmallows and melt, stirring constantly – be careful, they can burn very easily.

Remove from the heat and stir in the puffed rice. The mixture will be very thick and sticky. Pour into the prepared baking tray, flatten, and leave to cool and set. Once set, cut into ten portions and serve.

209 CALS / **3g** FAT / **0.9g** SAT FAT / **40.9g** SUGARS / **0.12g** SALT

FRIED BANANAS WITH RUM

Yes, it's true: fried bananas and ice cream in a book with 'diet' in the title! Well, why not? We are the Greedy Girls, after all!

SERVES 4

2 tablespoons reduced-fat butter
4 large, ripe bananas
juice of ½ lime
60g soft dark brown sugar
1 teaspoon ground cinnamon
½ teaspoon ground ginger
2 tablespoons rum

Preheat the oven to 200°C/Gas 6. Spread a little of the butter into a shallow baking tray – choose one small enough to let the bananas cuddle up to each other in one layer. Put the bananas in, pour the lime juice over them and then sprinkle them with the sugar and spices. Dot the rest of the butter on top and bake for about 10 minutes or until the bananas are soft and golden, then remove the pan from the oven.

Heat the rum in a small saucepan, pour it over the bananas and then set light to it. As soon as the flames have died down, serve with a little low-fat vanilla ice cream or cream.

I really believe it's important to have a little of what you fancy in order to avoid the dreaded binge.

UNDER **10** MINUTES
45 0 15 30

191 CALS / **12g** FAT / **0.9g** SAT FAT / **16.1g** SUGARS / **0.12g** SALT

VANILLA ICE CREAM, NUTS AND MAPLE SYRUP

Now wait for it, girls – you'll be eating your pud in a matter of seconds!

SERVES 4

4 scoops reduced-fat vanilla
  ice cream
20 pecans
4 tablespoons maple syrup

Line up four bowls and put a scoop of the ice cream in each one. Sprinkle five pecans into each bowl and then drizzle 1 tablespoon of maple syrup over each one.

Stop, put your feet up and enjoy.

10 MINUTES
45 0 15 30

176 CALS / **5g** FAT / **3.2g** SAT FAT / **11g** SUGARS / **1.03g** SALT

GOLDEN CRUMPETS AND CREAM

SERVES 4

4 crumpets
150ml reduced-fat cream
1 teaspoon good-quality vanilla
  extract
4 dessertspoons golden syrup

Grill the crumpets and, meanwhile, don't waste any time – put the cream and vanilla extract in a little bowl and whisk with an electric whisk until thickened.

By now, the crumpets should be ready. Spread them with the golden syrup and then top each one with a dollop of vanilla cream. Eat with an ever-so-dainty knife and fork.

HAPPY HALF HOUR

Delightful dinners in 30 minutes

MONDAY TO FRIDAY
(30-MINUTE MEALS)

The phrase 'Happy Hour' is something that should make us crazy with Friday night excitement; something to look forward to and work towards (rather than something to regret and look back upon with a sore head!).

So, with this in mind, and given the fact that the average prep time for a home-cooked evening meal is around an hour, I thought it would be a good idea to give us Greedy Girls back, if not a happy hour, then at least a Happy Half Hour.

How? Well, by simply creating lots of delicious dishes that take just half an hour to get on the table!

We all know how Greedy Girls are greedy for great food, but we also need to be a little greedier for time. Which is where the Happy Half Hour section comes in.

Hungry for food and now hungry for time! Time to lounge in a bath and drink gin, to wax your moustache, find a book, shave your legs, attempt to read a book, bleach your beard, finish your book,

clean the oven (noooooo!!!), write a love letter, consider a hobby, freak out to Abba's 'Dancing Queen', play with your kids, play with your fella...!

Time is in as short a supply as calories are in excess. Where we have to dodge the calories, we are forever trying to claw back the minutes. Busy girls lead busy lives. So, bring on the Happy Half Hour! A guilt-free gift from me to you!

After all, when do any of us ever get to actually stop the clock? Never. Well, here's the trade-off. Whenever you cook one of my Happy Half Hour dishes, you are instructed (no, ordered) to immediately give yourself the ultimate gift of half an hour of free time. It's yours! Not only will I have you saving calories, but I will also have you saving vital minutes. Just as precious, just as rewarding and, with the right attitude, just as tasty and fulfilling!

I order you to take your half hour hostage. Hold it close to your bosom like a lover and don't let anyone else you live

I thought it would be a good idea to give us Greedy Girls back, if not a happy hour, then at least a Happy Half Hour.

with take it away from you. It's yours to do with as you please.

Think of all those things you could do with impunity: knit a scarf, darn a sock (do people still do that!?), plant some plants, have a cry, phone your mum, dance, laugh, try singing, scream at the top of your voice, write a poem, give yourself a manicure, smoke a packet of fags, pay someone else to give you a manicure, rock in the fetal position whilst sucking your thumb, hoover, dust things off, sit and contemplate life, meditate, go for a run, slide on a slide, swing on a swing, draw a picture with your kids, do the kids' homework (much quicker than getting them to do it!), exfoliate everything, play the piano, clean the windows, stand on your head (very good for the brain), or take a nap.

So, Greedy Girls of the world, here is my attempt to give you back a little of your freedom as well as your waistlines!

281 CALS / **18g** FAT / **7.5g** SAT FAT / **4.3g** SUGARS / **0.35g** SALT

SPICED LEBANESE KEBABS

Having grown up in an Anglo-Arab family, this is the food of my childhood, so it naturally always puts me in a rather happy place. Nothing feels 'diety' about this dish – it's a real feast for the senses with all of its fabulous colours, tastes and smells.

SERVES 4

For the kebabs
500g lean minced lamb
1 teaspoon ground ginger
1 teaspoon allspice
1 teaspoon ground cinnamon
½ teaspoon ground black pepper
1 garlic clove, squished
zest of 1 unwaxed lemon

For the salad
1 green pepper, deseeded and chopped
4 tomatoes, chopped
small bunch of fresh flat-leaf parsley, finely chopped
small bunch of fresh mint, finely chopped
1 teaspoon sumac (optional)

For the dressing
juice of ½ lemon
½ tablespoon olive oil
½ teaspoon honey
good pinch of salt

To serve
4 wholemeal pitta breads or small tortillas

Heat the grill to medium heat, ready for the kebabs.

Put all the kebab ingredients into a bowl, mix well to break up the mince and combine, and then (you won't believe this, we're almost done!) mould the meat into eight flattish-looking sausage shapes (I know it sounds weird but look at the picture and you'll see what I mean).

Thread the meat onto metal or bamboo skewers (if you're using wooden skewers, remember to soak them in water first), pop them under the grill (a barbecue would be even better, but ho hum!) and while they're cooking, you can make the salad.

Simply put all the salad ingredients except the sumac into a large bowl. In a smaller bowl, whisk together the dressing ingredients. Drizzle the dressing over the salad and give it a good stir. To finish, sprinkle with the sumac if you fancy it!

Now it should be about time to turn over your kebabs and cook for another couple of minutes, so they'll have cooked for about 8 minutes in total. I like a little pinkness in the middle to keep them juicy, but it's up to you. Next heat the pitta breads or tortillas and serve stuffed with the spiced kebab and salad.

494 CALS / **11g** FAT / **3.1g** SAT FAT / **4.3g** SUGARS / **0.78g** SALT

PARMESAN CHICKEN

This is not only a family favourite (if only the kids knew it had 'smelly Parmesan' in it!) but also a vital weapon in my fearless fight against those demonic frozen chicken nuggets that kids across the world appear to worship! The girls prefer to have the Red Basghetti (page 20) rather than the herby potatoes alongside it, so I usually fold and get the pasta pot out! Grrr, bad mother!

SERVES 4

1kg new potatoes, halved
4 skinless chicken breast fillets
2 tablespoons plain flour
2 egg whites
4 tablespoons freshly grated
    Parmesan cheese
4 thin slices of wholemeal bread,
    made into breadcrumbs
1 tablespoon vegetable oil
1 tablespoon chopped chives
handful of your favourite fresh
    herbs
zest of 1 lemon
25g reduced-fat butter
salt and freshly ground black
    pepper

Salt the new potatoes and steam for 10–12 minutes until tender.

Sandwich the chicken breasts between two sheets of cling film and then use a rolling pin to bash them flat. Put the flour on a plate and season with salt and pepper. Put the egg whites in a shallow bowl and whisk them lightly. Then mix the Parmesan and breadcrumbs on another plate and season them well with salt and pepper.

Now dip those poor beaten up chicken breasts into the flour, then the egg whites and then into the breadcrumb and Parmesan mixture.

Heat the oil in a heavy-based frying pan over a medium heat and fry the chicken in two batches for a couple of minutes on each side until cooked through.

By now your potatoes should be ready. Combine the chives, your chosen herbs and lemon zest with the butter and then stir into the potatoes. Serve alongside the Parmesan chicken. I think a lovely mixed salad would be the perfect side dish.

365 CALS / **9g** FAT / **2g** SAT FAT / **12.9g** SUGARS / **0.51g** SALT

LEEKY CHICKEN PIE

Now this is my 'go-to' recipe when I am as miserable as sin and want to be comforted, or when it's a rainy day and I want to get cosy with the family, or when I am having friends over for mid-week supper, or... you get the picture, right? Leeky chicken pie is an amazing all-round recipe for every occasion!

SERVES 4

1 tablespoon vegetable oil
2 leeks, sliced
4 carrots, sliced
1 tablespoon plain flour
300ml skimmed milk
3 cooked chicken breasts, skin
  removed, cut into small chunks
handful of mushrooms, sliced
1 tablespoon chopped fresh sage
150g frozen petits pois
6 sheets filo pastry
olive oil spray
sea salt and freshly ground black
  pepper

Preheat the oven to 180°C/Gas 4.

Heat the oil in a non-stick frying pan over a medium heat. Add the leeks and carrots and fry until they are softened. Then sprinkle in the flour and stir it into the leeks and carrots for about a minute.

Gradually add in the milk, stirring the whole time, until the sauce is smooth. Add the chicken and mushrooms and bring up to the bubble. Turn the heat down, add the sage, and let everything simmer for several minutes until it thickens.

Now add the petits pois and give it all a good stir. Season well and then pour the gorgeous creamy chicken mix into an ovenproof dish. Scrunch up the filo pastry sheets and then layer on top of the chicken mixture. Spray with a little oil.

Pop into the oven and bake until the filo is golden, 8–10 minutes. Serve with steamed broccoli.

If you have leftover chicken from your Sunday roast it would work well in this recipe.

236 CALS / **5.4g** FAT / **0.8g** SAT FAT / **1.9g** SUGARS / **1.6g** SALT

STEAMED GINGER AND LEMONGRASS HALIBUT

This is my husband's favourite dish and he says he would eat it every day if he could. Well, even though it is delicious, if we had to eat it every day it would end in divorce! Variety is, after all, the spice of life!

SERVES 4

**4 lovely big pieces of fresh halibut
(or whatever firm white fish
you fancy)**
1 teaspoon sea salt
2 teaspoons sesame oil
10 thin slices of fresh ginger
**1 lemongrass stem, pale section
only, thinly sliced on the diagonal**
1 carrot, cut into thin strips
2 spring onions, finely sliced
2 tablespoons dry sherry
4 tablespoons chicken stock

Rub the fish pieces with the salt and sesame oil. Put them onto a plate and sprinkle with the ginger, lemongrass, carrot and spring onions.

Bring about 5cm of water to the boil in a medium wok or saucepan and then put a steamer basket in. It's important it fits neatly into the wok or saucepan you've chosen, to make sure the steam can't escape from the sides. You've also got to make sure the water doesn't touch the bottom of the steamer basket or you risk your food being poached rather than steamed. Reduce the heat to a medium–low heat so the water is just at a gentle bubble.

Put the plate of fish into the steamer basket. Pour over the sherry and stock and cover tightly with a lid. If you can't fit all the fish onto one plate, simply arrange bamboo skewers or chopsticks in a criss cross on the plate and then place another plate on top of the chopsticks, so that your plates are layered. Leave to steam very gently for 8–10 minutes. You will know the fish is cooked when it's firm to touch.

Serve with 5 or 6 tablespoons per person of cooked brown basmati rice and your favourite green vegetable.

501 CALS / **36g** FAT / **6.1g** SAT FAT / **4.4g** SUGARS / **0.35g** SALT

PISTACHIO AND PESTO CRUSTED SALMON
WITH WATERCRESS SALAD

This is a wonderful summery dish that's perfect for a girly lunch in the garden. By the way, did you know bubbly wine goes really well with salmon? Remember the Happy Half Hour promise!

SERVES 4

juice of ½ lemon (use the other ½
   for the dressing, below)
4 salmon fillets, roughly 150g each
3 tablespoons pesto
100g chopped pistachios

For the watercress salad
large bunch of watercress
4 sprigs fresh mint, finely chopped
handful of fresh flat-leaf parsley,
   chopped
2 handfuls of your favourite
   lettuce

For the dressing
zest and juice of ½ lemon
1 tablespoon olive oil
1 teaspoon honey
salt

Preheat the oven to 190°C/Gas 5.

Squeeze the lemon juice over the salmon fillets and then place them, skin-side down, on a baking tray. Spread the pesto (I always pour the excess oil off the top of the jar) over the top of each of those so-good-for-you-it's-untrue salmon fillets, then sprinkle each one equally with the pistachio nuts. Roast in the oven for 10–12 minutes.

Meanwhile, make the salad. Put the watercress, mint, parsley and lettuce into a bowl. Mix the salad dressing ingredients together in another bowl and drizzle over the salad.

When the salmon is ready, serve with the watercress salad and some steamed new potatoes. I cannot tell you how much better new potatoes taste when you steam rather than boil them.

667 CALS / **47g** FAT / **12g** SAT FAT / **13.7g** SUGARS / **4.25g** SALT

SMOKED MACKEREL, BEETROOT
AND POTATO SALAD

Oily fish brings with it the promise of gleaming hair, brilliant brain function and a million Brownie points. It also tastes rather good, especially with beets and horseradish!

SERVES 4

400g baby new potatoes, cut in half
200g green beans, trimmed
4 smoked mackerel fillets, skin removed
6 cooked beetroots, cut however you fancy
½ cucumber, cut into chunks
½ red onion, thinly sliced
large salad bowl full of your favourite leaves

For the dressing
100ml half-fat sour cream
1 tablespoon horseradish sauce
1 teaspoon Dijon mustard
zest of 1 lemon
1 teaspoon chopped fresh dill (optional)
1 teaspoon chopped fresh tarragon (optional)
salt and freshly ground black pepper

Place the potatoes in the bottom layer of a steamer over a saucepan of boiling water. After 5 minutes, place the green beans in the second layer of the steamer and cover. Steam until tender, about another 3–4 minutes.

Meanwhile, make the dressing by mixing all the lovely dressing ingredients together. Lots of black pepper is a must here!

When the potatoes and green beans are cooked, run under cold water to cool them down quickly (this means you get to eat sooner!). Tip them into a large bowl and pour half the dressing over them so it can soak in a bit.

Flake the mackerel into the bowl with the potatoes and beans. Add the beetroots, cucumber, onion and salad leaves. Mix together and serve, drizzled with the remaining dressing.

324 CALS / 5g FAT / 0.6g SAT FAT / 4.4g SUGARS / 0.26g SALT

LINGUINE VONGOLE

Mmm, slippery garlicky linguine with sweet-tasting (and -looking) baby clams enriched in ripe cherry tomato and wine sauce... leave me now, I'm in heaven...

SERVES 4

300g linguine
1 tablespoon olive oil
2 garlic cloves, sliced
handful of cherry tomatoes,
　halved
800g small clams, cleaned
　(I sometimes use tinned clams
　and they're fine)
125ml white wine
4 tablespoons finely chopped
　fresh flat-leaf parsley
zest of 1 lemon
salt

Cook the linguine according to packet instructions in lots of salty boiling water.

Meanwhile, heat the oil in a large frying pan over a medium heat. Fry the garlic for 30 seconds, then add the tomatoes. Cook for a few minutes, then throw in the clams, add the wine and stir. Cover with a lid and let it all cook for a couple of minutes.

Remove any clams that don't open – you shouldn't eat them! When the linguine is cooked, drain and toss in the pan with the clams and sauce. Sprinkle over the parsley and lemon zest and serve with a large salad.

QUICK TIPS

Even if you want to cook quickly, stretch out the act of eating for as long as possible and you're less likely to feel hungry later. Adding a large salad to this meal means you can linger longer at the table, relishing every mouthful.

354 CALS / 13g FAT / 2g SAT FAT / 4.6g SUGARS / 0.78g SALT

SWORDFISH AND COUSCOUS

I'm going to be honest with you here. I don't actually (shock-gasp-horror) like couscous very much! But, I am the only person I've ever met who doesn't, so I've very kindly added it to this recipe! I'll have rice with mine, though, if you don't mind...

SERVES 4

200g couscous
4 swordfish steaks
20 small vine tomatoes, quartered
20 black olives in brine, drained
small bunch of fresh flat-leaf
  parsley, chopped
4 tablespoons finely chopped fresh
  mint
3 spring onions, finely chopped
salt and freshly ground black
  pepper

For the dressing
zest and juice of 1 lemon
1 teaspoon pesto
1 tablespoon olive oil
½ teaspoon honey

Cook the couscous according to the packet instructions, making sure you season the water.

Heat the grill to medium, season the swordfish and cook for about 4 minutes on each side. Put the tomatoes in a bowl with the olives, parsley, mint, spring onions and drained couscous (if you have used easy-cook couscous, it won't need draining – just fluff it up with a fork).

Mix together the dressing ingredients, pour over the couscous salad and serve with the grilled swordfish.

CHILLI CON CARNE COTTAGE PIE

I have never met a single person who makes chilli con carne and doesn't believe that their version is the best in the world! So, here's mine – and it really is the best one ever because... I have rather wickedly added mash to the game!

SERVES 4

450g lean beef, cut into strips
   (I like to use sirloin)
1 teaspoon ground cumin
1 teaspoon ground allspice
1 teaspoon ground coriander
1 or 2 fresh red chillies, chopped
2 garlic cloves, finely chopped
1 tablespoon vegetable oil
1 large onion, finely chopped
625g thick passata
1 tablespoon tomato purée
200g tinned kidney beans,
   drained
100ml beef stock (optional)
2 bay leaves
800g potatoes, peeled and
   chopped into even-sized
   chunks
2 tablespoons crème fraîche
small handful of chopped fresh
   coriander
salt

Put the beef into a bowl and mix with the ground spices, chillies and the garlic and give it all a good stir.

Heat a heavy-based pan over a medium heat and dry-fry the beef for a couple of minutes. Set to one side. In the same pan, heat the oil and fry the onion until softened. Throw the meat back in, pour in the passata, tomato purée and kidney beans and, if you think it needs it, some beef stock. Add the bay leaves and bring to the boil, then reduce the heat and leave to simmer for 15 minutes.

Meanwhile, boil your potatoes in salted water until tender, then drain and mash with the crème fraîche and some chopped fresh coriander.

Put your chilli con carne into an ovenproof dish, top with the potatoes and then pop under a hot grill until golden.

Serve with steamed veg.

572 CALS / **37g** FAT / **17.2g** SAT FAT / **4.1g** SUGARS / **0.99g** SALT

GARLIC SPICED LAMB WITH HARICOT BEANS

This makes a great dinner party treat and never fails to impress. It's a fabulous dish if you have carnivores and vegetarians (just double up on the beans and spices) sharing the same table with you, because we have those two top ingredients present that can keep both sides of the foody divide happy: lamb and beans!

SERVES 4

For the lamb spice rub
1 teaspoon paprika
1 teaspoon ground coriander
1 teaspoon ground cumin
sea salt and freshly ground black
   pepper

rack of 12 lamb chops, sliced into
   chops
1 tablespoon olive oil
1 medium onion, finely chopped
70g smoked bacon, all visible fat
   removed, chopped
2 garlic cloves, sliced
handful of cherry tomatoes
400g tin haricot beans, drained
100ml white wine
small bunch of fresh coriander,
   finely chopped

Get the grill nice and hot. Whilst that's heating, mix the spice rub ingredients together and then, yes, you guessed it, rub the mix into the lamb chops. Pop them under the grill and cook on both sides for 4 minutes until crispy on the outside and pleasantly pink in the middle.

Now it's time to prepare your beautiful beans. Heat the oil in a heavy-based, non-stick frying pan over a medium heat. Add the onion and cook. Once it's softened, add your bacon and garlic and cook for another minute, stirring. Now throw in the baby tomatoes, haricot beans and white wine. Bring up to the bubble, then keep the heat nice and low and simmer for 5–10 minutes, so that all the flavours can infuse the beans.

Finally, stir in the chopped coriander and serve with the lamb chops.

356 CALS / **8g** FAT / **2.2g** SAT FAT / **3.4g** SUGARS / **0.36g** SALT

SAUSAGE PATTIES WITH CHAMP
AND RED WINE GRAVY

Don't get me wrong – like any Greedy Girl, I love a traditional sausage. The problem is, I can never be sure exactly what's in them. Let's face it, it's usually tons of fat and rusk! That's why I love to make these 'oh so good for you' sausage patties and have full control over what goes into them! Control freak!

Champ is an Irish potato dish that's the perfect partner to these sausage patties. Let's face it girls, what the Irish DON'T know about potatoes isn't worth knowing.

SERVES 4

For the sausage patties
1 teaspoon reduced-fat butter or olive oil
1 leek, finely chopped
500g lean pork, finely minced
3 tablespoons cooked brown rice
a little freshly chopped sage
zest of 1 lemon
salt and freshly ground black pepper

For the champ
800g floury potatoes, such as King Edward or Maris Piper, peeled and chopped into even-sized chunks
140ml skimmed milk
70g spring onions, finely chopped
1 tablespoon reduced-fat butter

Start by boiling the potatoes in plenty of salted water for 15–20 minutes.

Meanwhile, heat the butter or oil in a frying pan and cook the leek until softened, then mix with the rest of the patty ingredients in a large bowl.

Preheat the grill to medium. Wet your hands and use them to form eight equal-sized sausage patties. Cook the patties under the grill for 6–8 minutes until they are cooked through.

Put the milk and spring onions into a small pan, bring up to the bubble and then take off the heat and allow to infuse. Once the potatoes are tender, drain really well and then mash with the butter and spring onion milk (sounds disgusting but I promise it isn't). Season with salt and pepper and serve with the sausage patties.

As always, serve with your favourite salad leaves or veg.

STEAK STICKS AND ASIAN SALAD

Feel free to use lamb, chicken or indeed fish instead of steak in this recipe. The flavours would work well with any of them. I think a little bowl of rice or noodles would be rather lovely too. After all, we don't want to go hungry, do we?!

SERVES 4

2 teaspoons five spice powder
2 teaspoons sesame seeds
1 garlic clove, crushed
1 tablespoon sweet chilli sauce
400g rump steak (all fat removed), cut into strips

For the salad
400g cabbage, shredded
½ cucumber, halved, seeded and sliced
2 carrots, grated
3 spring onions, finely sliced
50g dry roasted peanuts, chopped
handful of fresh mint leaves

For the dressing
1 teaspoon sesame oil (optional)
1 tablespoon rice wine vinegar
2 tablespoons Thai fish sauce (nam pla – sounds weird, but add it anyway!)
1 tablespoon sweet chilli sauce

Heat up your griddle pan or grill until it's really nice and hot. Whilst it's heating up, mix up the five spice powder, sesame seeds, garlic and chilli sauce in a bowl. Add the steak and give it all a good mix together.

Thread the steak strips onto metal or bamboo skewers (if you're using wooden skewers, remember to soak them in water first) and griddle or grill for 2–3 minutes on each side.

Put the prepared salad vegetables into a large bowl with the peanuts and mint leaves.

Now make the lovely salad dressing by mixing the sesame oil (if using), vinegar, Thai fish sauce and chilli sauce in a small bowl.

Toss the dressing into the salad and serve with the steak strips.

119 CALS / 5g FAT / 0.5g SAT FAT / 10.5g SUGARS / 0.09g SALT

AUBERGINE AND SPINACH CURRY

People will often turn their backs on the rude delights of the aubergine, especially when they're on a weight-loss mission, simply because they know that they absorb so much fat when fried and, let's face it, fried is the tastiest way to eat an aubergine! But the way I cook them in this dish works really well and they do indeed end up tasting fried – without actually being fried!

SERVES 4

3 aubergines, cut into small cubes
olive oil spray
1 tablespoon vegetable oil
1 large onion, chopped
2 garlic cloves, finely chopped
2 teaspoons dried coriander
1 teaspoon ground cumin
2 green chillies (you can use red
    if you prefer)
2cm piece of fresh ginger, grated
4 fresh tomatoes, chopped
large bag of baby leaf spinach (buy
    it washed, life's too short to wash
    spinach properly)
2 tablespoons chopped fresh
    coriander
salt and freshly ground black
    pepper

Preheat the oven to its highest setting.

Lay out the aubergine on two baking trays. Spray with olive oil, sprinkle with salt and pepper and put into the oven until lightly golden (about 10 minutes).

While your aubergine is browning, heat the vegetable oil in a heavy-based pan. Fry the onion, garlic, dried coriander, cumin, chillies and ginger until the onion is softened. Throw in your tomatoes and 3–4 tablespoons water and keep stirring.

Add your aubergine and cook for another few minutes, still stirring, and then finally add your spinach and coriander and cook until the spinach just wilts. It's now ready to serve.

123 CALS / **4g** FAT / **1.6g** SAT FAT / **1.9g** SUGARS / **0.87g** SALT

MOULES, MARVELLOUS MOULES

To make this really speedy, make sure you buy your mussels already prepared, with barnacles scraped off, beards shaved and shells nice and clean.

SERVES 4

2 shallots, finely chopped
1 bay leaf
150ml dry white wine
1.5kg prepared mussels
2 teaspoons reduced-fat butter
small bunch of flat-leaf parsley,
   finely chopped
salt and freshly ground black
   pepper

Put the shallots, bay leaf and wine into a large, heavy-based pan and bring up to a bubble. Turn the heat down and simmer for 10 minutes so that the wine gets nicely infused with the flavours of the shallots and bay leaf. Now turn up the heat to medium and throw your mussels into the pan. Cover those babies and cook until most of them have opened – this should take 2–3 minutes.

Now add the butter (life's not worth living without butter) and put the lid back on until the butter melts. Discard any mussels that haven't opened. Add the parsley, give it all a good shake, season and – this is the best bit – eat it immediately with a lovely green salad!

152 CALS / **10g** FAT / **2.2g** SAT FAT / **4.2g** SUGARS / **0.6g** SALT

MOROCCAN TOMATO EGGS

Pleeease try this recipe, it really is utterly delicious! The first time I ever ate something like it (although it was much more fattening than this version) was in the spice market in downtown Marrakech and I've been hooked ever since. Feel free to play around with the spices. Allow yourself a slice or two of bread with it to mop up all the gorgeous spicy sauce. And of course a green salad would be marvellous served alongside.

SERVES 4

1 tablespoon olive oil
1 onion, diced
1 garlic clove, crushed (optional)
½ teaspoon ground cumin
½ teaspoon ground coriander
¼ teaspoon ground cinnamon
¼ teaspoon ground ginger
300g passata
small handful of fresh coriander,
   chopped
4 large eggs
salt and freshly ground black
   pepper

Preheat the oven to 220°C/Gas 7.

Heat the oil in a heavy-based frying pan. Add the onion and fry really slowly (this is a good time to use a diffuser). Once it's nice and soft, add your garlic and spices. Fry for a minute or so until the aroma is released.

Pour in the passata, season well and then turn the gas down to a gentle bubble and allow the sauce to pop away for 8–10 minutes. If it all starts to look a bit too thick, splash in a little water. Stir in your chopped coriander and pour the sauce into an ovenproof ceramic dish.

Gently crack the eggs into the sauce and cook in the oven for 8–10 minutes: 8 if you like them a little runny, 10 if you don't. But then again, that could all be utter nonsense depending on how efficient your oven is, so just keep checking towards the end.

Divide between four plates or bowls, making sure there is an egg in each, and serve with a green salad and some brown bread.

265 CALS / **11g** FAT / **7.7g** SAT FAT / **1.7g** SUGARS / **0.61g** SALT

THAI GREEN CURRY

Most people love Thai Green Curry – full of those gorgeous spices, fragrant with lemongrass and coriander, and rich with coconut milk. But, unfortunately, most Thai Green curries are extremely fattening, so I've come up with this slashed-calorie version, which I promise you faithfully is authentic-tasting and utterly delicious.

SERVES 4

1 tablespoon chopped fresh ginger

2 garlic cloves, roughly chopped

1 small onion, roughly chopped

2 green chillies, roughly chopped

1 teaspoon lemongrass paste, or two sticks lemongrass

1 teaspoon ground coriander

½ tablespoon olive or vegetable oil

400ml half-fat coconut milk

4 skinless chicken breasts, cut into small pieces

a good shake or two of fish sauce (nam pla)

zest and juice of 1 lime

bunch of fresh coriander, finely chopped

Put the ginger, garlic, onion, chillies, lemongrass and ground coriander in a food processor and whizz until you get a nice spicy paste.

Heat the oil in a large pan over a medium heat and fry the paste for 5 minutes until the aroma of the ginger, garlic and spices is released. Now pour the coconut milk into the pan and bring up to the bubble for a minute.

Add the chicken and simmer over a low heat for another 5–10 minutes until the chicken is cooked through (but be careful not to overcook).

Stir in the fish sauce and lime zest and juice. Scatter over the coriander and serve with steamed brown basmati rice and piles of energy-giving green veg!

When dieting, many people make the mistake of assuming that there are whole lists of favourite foods that they just can't eat any more. Rubbish! You just need to get creative. Tweak the ingredients and you'll soon see you don't need to miss out at all.

273 CALS / **12g** FAT / **4.2g** SAT FAT / **7g** SUGARS / **1.67g** SALT

ROCKET, HAM AND OLIVE PIZZAS

Even though I don't believe in cutting anything out of our diet completely, I'm afraid takeaway pizzas are so calorie-laden that we might just have to... but never fear, the Cheat's Pizzas are here. We simply cannot live without pizza, can we?

SERVES 4

4 small wholemeal tortilla wraps
olive oil spray
2 x 400g tins of chopped
  tomatoes, drained
4 slices Parma ham or speck (all
  fat removed)
100g low-fat mozzarella, sliced
4 tablespoons grated Parmesan
  cheese
20 black olives, pitted and halved
handful of rocket leaves (or basil
  if you prefer)
salt and freshly ground black
  pepper

Preheat the oven to 180°C/Gas 4.

Lay out the tortillas on two baking trays and spray them with olive oil.

Now share equally between the four tortillas the tomatoes (season them), then the ham, cheeses and olives. Bake in the oven until the cheeses are gorgeously melty, about 8–10 minutes.

Serve topped with the rocket/basil. Mmmm, glass of red anyone?

383 CALS / **8g** FAT / **3.8g** SAT FAT / **5g** SUGARS / **1.43g** SALT

VERY PRETTY PASTA

Could anything in the world be easier than this dish that does exactly what it says on the packet by being, put simply, 'Very Pretty Pasta'?

SERVES 4

150g smoked bacon, all fat
  removed, diced
300g pasta shapes of your choice
100g frozen peas
75ml low-fat cream
75ml low-fat crème fraîche
2 tablespoons grated Parmesan
  cheese
salt

Dry-fry the bacon until crisp and set aside.

Cook the pasta according to the packet instructions in lots and lots of salty water. In the last few minutes of cooking time, throw in the peas.

Once the pasta and peas are cooked, drain them well and put them back into the pasta pan. Mix together the cream and crème fraîche in a bowl and then pour into the pan along with the bacon and Parmesan, making sure they all warm through, and serve.

Eating is about so much more than the act of shoving food in your gob. It's about flavour, texture and aroma, and it's also very visual. So try to create beautiful-looking dishes like this one – you'll enjoy them all the more.

431 CALS / **4g** FAT / **1.2g** SAT FAT / **11.3g** SUGARS / **0.14g** SALT

MEDITERRANEAN VEGETABLE PASTA

This is one of those pasta dishes that, if you made a huge bowl of it, would be just as lovely cold the next day in your packed lunch. It also works rather well if you are allowing vegetarians and carnivores to meet at the same barbecue!

SERVES 4

1 aubergine, cubed
2 courgettes, cubed
2 red peppers, deseeded and cubed
4 garlic cloves, chopped
15 baby tomatoes on the vine
olive oil spray
2 sprigs each of oregano and
   thyme (you can use dried herbs
   instead, but they don't taste as
   nice)
400g pasta shapes of your choice
2 tablespoons grated Parmesan
   cheese
sea salt and freshly ground black
   pepper

Preheat the oven to 200°C/Gas 6.

Put all the vegetables and tomatoes in a roasting tin, spray with olive oil and season with lots of sea salt and freshly ground pepper. Then sprinkle with the oregano and thyme and roast in the oven for 20 minutes.

Meanwhile, cook the pasta according to the packet instructions in lots and lots of salty water. Once the pasta is cooked, drain it well and pop it back into the pasta pan.

Stir in your roasted vegetables, dish up between four bowls and then sprinkle equal amounts of Parmesan on the top before serving.

550 CALS / **16g** FAT / **6.2g** SAT FAT / **4.6g** SUGARS / **1.84g** SALT

BRING ON THE CARBS CARBONARA

Whenever I went on a diet that demanded that I gave up carbs, I would eventually (usually after only a couple of days) end up behaving like a deranged bloodthirsty murderer... not a pretty sight. So now I simply never have a meal without carbs – hoorah!

SERVES 4

400g spaghetti (this is not an occasion for wholemeal spaghetti!)
2 teaspoons olive oil
6 rashers back bacon, cubed, all fat removed
70g grated Parmesan cheese
5 tablespoons low-fat crème fraîche
3 egg yolks
1 teaspoon coarsely ground black pepper
2 tablespoons chopped fresh flat-leaf parsley
salt

Sorry, but here I go again – cook the spaghetti according to the packet instructions in plenty of salty water.

Heat the oil in a non-stick frying pan over a medium heat and fry the bacon until it browns slightly. Mix together the Parmesan, crème fraîche, egg yolks and black pepper. Add this mixture to the pan.

Stir in the cooked, drained spaghetti and top with the parsley. Serve with a rocket salad.

QUICK TIPS

It's easy to make the mistake of thinking that you shouldn't have carbs when you're on a diet, but trying to cut out an entire food group will just make you crave it even more. So, as I've said before – have a little of what you fancy!

118 CALS / **5g** FAT / **0.6g** SAT FAT / **6.5g** SUGARS / **0.63g** SALT

TASTETASTIC CHICKPEA AND CORIANDER TAGINE

Jump up onto my magic carpet and fly with me to Morocco for a magical supper. I assure you, you may never want to return... This dish is best made in a tagine, but if you don't have one, a heavy-based pan will do.

SERVES 4

1½ tablespoons olive oil
2 onions, finely chopped
4 garlic cloves, chopped
1 teaspoon ground cumin
1 teaspoon ground cinnamon
1 teaspoon ground coriander
1 teaspoon ground turmeric
1 cinnamon stick
400g tin plum tomatoes
100g tinned chickpeas, drained
200ml chicken stock
handful of fresh coriander or
    flat-leaf parsley, chopped
a pinch of sugar (optional)
sea salt and freshly ground black
    pepper

Heat the oil slowly in your tagine or heavy-based pan. Add the onions and garlic and fry until soft (the finer you've chopped the onions, the better – don't forget we're doing this against the clock!).

Add all the spices and stir for about a minute or until the aromas are released. Now add the tomatoes (don't break up the tomatoes with the spoon, however tempted you are; I think this works better if they are kept whole), the chickpeas and the stock. Bring up to the bubble, reduce the heat and let it all cook away for 20 minutes. Sprinkle over the coriander or parsley.

Taste before serving and adjust the seasoning, adding a pinch of sugar only if the sauce is tasting a little sharp.

You can make this a more substantial meal by adding a few tablespoons of rice or quinoa.

478 CALS / **11g** FAT / **3.7g** SAT FAT / **3.8g** SUGARS / **1.07g** SALT

BROCCOLI, CHILLI, GARLIC AND EARS

My big sister, Dina, lived in southern Italy for a year (ah, jealousy will get me nowhere) and came back with so many wonderfully simple but utterly delicious pasta dishes, like this one, that we crowned her our pasta queen!

SERVES 4

300g sprouting broccoli
400g orecchiette pasta (which in
    Italian means 'little ears'!)
2 tablespoons olive oil
3 garlic cloves, finely sliced
1 red chilli, finely chopped
50g grated Pecorino cheese
salt

Bring a large saucepan of salted water to the boil. Throw the broccoli in for a minute, then take it out with a slotted spoon and put it to one side.

Now throw the orecchiette into the same water and boil according to packet instructions until it's tender.

Meanwhile, heat the olive oil in a frying pan over a medium heat. When it's hot, fry the garlic until it's just starting to turn golden (don't burn it, though, or you'll have to chuck it), then add the chilli and stir for another 30 seconds.

Drain the orecchiette and add it to the pan with the chilli and garlic. Stir in the broccoli. Give it all a good mix and serve, scattered with the grated Pecorino.

PISTACHIO PLUM POCKETS

These sweet stuffed plums are so easy to make and look so pretty that your guests will simply fall in love with you. Okay, we all know I'm prone to a little exaggeration...

SERVES 4

115g low-fat soft cheese
1 tablespoon light muscovado sugar
2 tablespoons ground pistachios
8 large firm plums, halved and stoned
8 sheets filo pastry
2 tablespoons melted low-fat spread
icing sugar, for dusting

Preheat the oven to 230°C/Gas 8.

Mix together the soft cheese, muscovado sugar and ground pistachios to make a firm paste.

Fill the stoned plums with the pistachio paste and then sandwich each pair of plum halves together.

Stack the filo sheets and cut in half so that you have 16 pieces, each 23cm square. Brush one slice with some of the melted spread and place another diagonally on top. Repeat with the rest so that you have 8 pretty shapes.

Place your beautifully stuffed plums on each filo pastry shape, lift up the sides and pinch the corners together.

Put them on a baking sheet and bake for 15 minutes or until nicely golden. Dust with a little icing sugar before serving.

You can swap the plums here for peaches or nectarines, if you like.

201 CALS / **3g** FAT / **0g** SAT FAT / **38.1g** SUGARS / **0.19g** SALT

BEAUTIFUL BAKED ALASKA

I almost feel embarrassed at how easy this is to make compared to how beautiful it looks and how heavenly it tastes. Of course it goes without saying that you don't need to breathe a word to your friends and family about how easy it is. Just sit back (for that extra half hour you've just gained) and lap up the applause!

SERVES 6

2 egg whites
100g caster sugar
1 frozen Arctic Roll
lots of your favourite berries

Preheat the oven to 230°C/Gas 8.

Make the meringue by whisking the egg whites with an electric whisk to stiff peaks, then gradually whisk in the sugar a spoonful at a time.

Place the Arctic Roll on a baking tray lined with non-stick baking paper and pipe or slather the meringue over the Arctic Roll. Bake for 10 minutes, or until the meringue is golden brown.

Obviously, serve immediately, along with the berries, which add that extra flash of beauty!

QUICK TIPS

Serving desserts like this with a heap of fresh berries on the side ensures you get plenty of goodness with your little bit of naughtiness.

157 CALS / **0g** FAT / **0g** SAT FAT / **29.9g** SUGARS / **0.44g** SALT

STRAWBERRY ANGEL CAKE

Can you hear the angels singing? Well, you should do, because this cake is so light in texture and calories that the angels just love it! Now I'm cheating a little bit here, because this recipe takes a little longer than half an hour – but as you can spend the whole time that it's baking in the oven just relaxing, I felt I had to include it!

SERVES 12

12 egg whites
1 teaspoon cream of tartar
seeds from 2 vanilla pods
300g caster sugar
115g plain flour
¼ teaspoon salt

For the topping
300g small, sweet
  strawberries

Preheat the oven to 180°C/Gas 4. Grease and line a 25-cm angel cake tin.

Using a free-standing whisk, beat the egg whites on medium speed until they are foamy. Then sprinkle in the cream of tartar and beat again, but this time you are after soft peaks. Now add the vanilla seeds and sugar, one spoonful at a time, whisking all the while, until you have stiff peaks and all the sugar has been incorporated.

Mix the flour and salt together and then sift half of it on top of the egg white mixture. Fold in gently with a metal spoon, using a figure of eight motion – you don't want to beat out all the air you have just so carefully put in. Repeat with the rest of the flour.

Now really carefully spoon your sponge mix into the tin and bake in the oven for 40–45 minutes or until the sponge is a light golden colour. Let the cake cool completely in the tin, then run a palette knife round the edge to loosen it. Serve with the strawberries piled on top.

If you want to adapt this recipe, you could swap the strawberries for a blackberry sauce. Simply put 200g blackberries and 2 tablespoons caster sugar in a small pan and bring up to the bubble, then simmer for 8–10 minutes. Let it cool before pouring over the angel cake.

GREEDY GIRLS ON THE MOVE

Spectacular soups and sandwiches for the perfect packed lunch

GREEDY GIRLS ON THE MOVE

Now I don't want to irritate you all by banging on about what a brilliant thing it is to pack our own lunches every day, but I'm going to anyway! Why? Because I really want us to get that dastardly weight off – and I want us to keep it off! The thing about eating is that it is something that creeps up on us. It's sneaky. It's something that we HAVE to do, and because of this simple fact, it's difficult to keep a lid on it. And yet, somehow, a Tupperware lid seems like a very appropriate barrier to putting on weight at that dangerous time of the working day – lunch.

The other reason I want to home in on our work lunches is because I also want us to feel as energised and nourished as we possibly can after eating them, rather than the usual feelings of guilt mixed in with food coma and, over time, rolls of flab and flesh that resemble a bap more than a waistline!

So, in order to avoid this very particular form of homphing hell, I feel that stealthily heading out into the cruel world (quite literally brimming with temptation at every street corner) with our very own Tupperware hand-grenade in our bag is not only a must, but is, in fact, every Greedy Girl's duty! If we're not prepared from the off, we must inevitably prepare to fail (that's some other genius's line by the way, not mine!). I promise, all the recipes below take the minimum preparation!

I know, I know. You're already thinking: 'That's all well and good, Nads. But it's already hard enough to get everyone out of the door in the morning without faffing around trying to make lunch for myself!'

Trust me, I know how you feel. I'm in this terrified state every morning of my life. Just this morning, for instance, it was utter carnage in my house. I had to cut chewing gum out of my youngest's hair (don't ask!), test my 10-year-old on her times tables (she hasn't got a clue I don't know them myself!), help my husband find his car keys (three times!), feed the guinea pigs, walk the dog, sew a button and a name tag on a school blazer, search for a lost plimsoll (I didn't find it), dye my roots (big meeting later) and search through 20 pairs of tights to find a pair

pair with only a small ladder (I knew, deep in my soul, there wasn't one to be found!). So, factoring in the time to make my packed lunch felt like a task too far! But I did it, and here's why.

In the bad old days (when I was three stone heavier and even walking around the kitchen made me breathless) on a morning like the one I've just described, the packed lunch would, without a doubt, have been the first thing to bite the dust! But, now that I'm older and wiser, I know only too well the danger I would put myself in if I went to work without my OWN food!!

I use the word 'danger' purposefully, because if I venture into the world unarmed with a healthy, delicious, filling meal then, dread of all dreads, I would be left utterly vulnerable to the annoyingly enviable eating habits of the 'skinny cows'! You know the kind of girls I'm talking about. The kind that say: 'Oh ... I forgot to have lunch today.'

FORGOT TO HAVE LUNCH?! I've never forgotten a meal in my entire life – whether it's a meal I've had, or a meal I want!

The kind of 'skinny' that can eat nothing for hours, and then consumes enough calories to keep a hippo happy for months – without even the slightest bulge appearing anywhere... ever! (Though I have to say, that if you take a look at them next time they're gorging their skinny little faces, just observe how they never quite clean their plates!)

The kind of woman who says annoying things like, 'Oh – no thanks.

I'm not hungry today. I went out to dinner last night.'

Sorry? Are you serious? What's last night's dinner got to do with the oasis of food I want to consume today?! If I'd been out to dinner the night before, it would invariably be as a means of research to find out what I could be eating tonight that could fill me up even more!

They say things like, 'I don't know what it is, but whenever I go to the gym in the morning I don't feel hungry all day.'

You know. The kind of comment that makes you want to consider murder.

Comments like these are bad enough for us mere mortal Greedy Girls, but it's when these throwaway lines are followed by those days when they DO eat that life becomes unbearable and it's clearly time to call the men in white coats. When the skinny girls decide to eat, boy do they go at it with gusto; usually a never-ending stream of the most fattening things possible, which they seem to consume and consume and consume willy-nilly, but in truth usually leave half of! Mugs of milky coffee, boxes of jam doughnuts, giant chocolate cookies and – one of the greatest insults of all to the 'fuller-figured girl' – they crack open a can of FULL SUGAR COKE! Ahh! The cows!!! The skinny bitches!!! Is there no end to their cruelty!?!

And as if this wasn't enough, they're so flaming generous with their food! Offering STUFF to everyone else ALL day! I mean, Christ, if they don't want it, why don't they just throw it in the flaming bin?! In fact, my theory on the skinnies is that they purposefully eat their food in front of Greedy Girls, and deliberately offer it around so that they end up having nothing to eat themselves at all! It's a kind of dieting sabotage! They're size 8 suicide bombers , tricking all of us Greedy Girls into a nibble here and a nibble there! They lure us in to their skinny orbit and fool us with their 'pretend' gorge by letting US eat everything! It's a tactic! It's a plan! It's a conspiracy! They're WMDDs! Women of Mass Dieting Destruction!

Skinny Cow says: 'Pizza, anyone? I can't eat another mouthful – I'm stuffed.'

Greedy Girl thinks: 'Yessssssss!'

Skinny Cow says: 'Anyone want anything from the bakery?'

Greedy Girl thinks: 'YES, EVERYTHING!'

Skinny Cow shouts: 'I've brought in cupcakes for everyone.'

Greedy Girl thinks: 'Load me a gun!'

So. Step away from the gun, girls... and step towards your very own packed lunches. Packed with goodness, packed with flavour and packed with a one-fingered salute to skinny cows the world over!

20 MINUTES

127 CALS / **6g** FAT / **0.4g** SAT FAT / **7.2g** SUGARS / **1.51g** SALT

CURRIED CAULIFLOWER SOUP

This is wonderfully low in calories – and in cost – and is super easy to make... I curtsey to your applause.

SERVES 4

1 tablespoon olive oil
1 medium onion, chopped
1 garlic clove, chopped
1 tablespoon curry powder
1 large cauliflower, broken into small florets
750ml chicken or vegetable stock
freshly ground black pepper

Heat the oil in a heavy-based saucepan and fry the onion, garlic, curry powder and some freshly ground black pepper until the onion is softened.

Add the cauliflower, cover with the stock, and bring up to the bubble. Reduce the heat and simmer until the cauliflower is tender – about 10 minutes.

Blitz in a blender to your desired consistency and serve.

QUICK TIPS

Why not add some dry-fried nigella seeds and fresh coriander to this lovely spicy soup? Simply fry the nigella seeds in a dry, very hot, non-stick pan until they pop a little, and then scatter over the soup with the coriander.

121 CALS / **7g** FAT / **0.9g** SAT FAT / **12.5g** SUGARS / **0.07g** SALT

GAZPACHO

This is a great summer soup that you could have alongside any of the sandwiches or salads here, but please don't even think about making it unless you are going to use the most fabulous tomatoes available to mankind.

SERVES 2

230g cucumbers, chopped into rough chunks
450g good-quality tomatoes, chopped
20 basil leaves
1 small, sweet red pepper, deseeded and chopped
1 garlic clove, chopped (optional)
2 spring onions, sliced
1 tablespoon sherry vinegar
1 tablespoon olive oil
salt and white pepper, to taste

This is really simple, girls. Just put all the ingredients in a blender and whizz it up until smooth – or, of course, until it's chunky. Whichever you prefer – it's your lunch! Serve chilled.

If you are eating this at home, chop some extra cucumber, red pepper and onions to scatter on top, Spanish-style.

131 CALS / **5g** FAT / **0.4g** SAT FAT / **5.1g** SUGARS / **1.19g** SALT

MOROCCAN SOUP

Mmm. Spicy, hot and filling – the perfect winter warmer.

SERVES 4-6

1 tablespoon olive oil

1 onion, finely chopped (or grated
   if there's no time!)

2 celery sticks (not essential, but
   does add flavour)

1 teaspoon cumin

1 teaspoon ground coriander

1 teaspoon harissa (or chilli paste)

400g tin chickpeas, drained

400g tin chopped tomatoes

500ml hot stock (chicken, lamb
   or veg)

large handful of fresh coriander,
   finely chopped (optional)

Heat the oil in a large saucepan over a medium heat and
fry the onion, celery and spices until softened.

Add all the other ingredients and bring up to the bubble.
Reduce the heat and simmer for 10 minutes.

Now simply pour into your flask and you're good to go...
why not take a small hunk of bread with you to dip?

*Soup is the perfect comfort food,
especially when you're watching your
weight – it's quick and easy, a great way
to pack in the veg, and it leaves you
feeling full and satisfied.*

131 CALS / 5g FAT / 0.6g SAT FAT / 8.4g SUGARS / 3.16g SALT

SUPER DOOPER SOUP

Now, lots of people might look at these recipes and think, surely you don't need oil in a soup – but I think it is imperative! If you just boil veg in stock it really doesn't taste very nice. Simple as that. So, if sautéing the veg in a little oil takes the soup from being rather dull to rather yummy, why not?!

SERVES 4–6

1 tablespoon olive oil
1 medium onion, chopped
2 garlic cloves, chopped
½ head of celery, chopped
1 head of broccoli, chopped into
   florets and stalk also chopped
1 small pointed cabbage, chopped
2 Knorr chicken stock pots
1 mug petits pois

Heat the oil in a large saucepan over a low heat. Gently cook the onion, garlic and celery until really nice and soft but NOT browned.

Add the chopped broccoli stalk, cook for a few minutes and then add the florets and cabbage. Pour in 1.5 litres boiling water and the stock pots and cook for a couple of minutes, then add the petits pois and cook until they are just tender.

QUICK TIPS

Life is too short to weigh peas!
So just use a mug, like I do!

341 CALS / **9g** FAT / **2.5g** SAT FAT / **6.7g** SUGARS / **3.08g** SALT

SMOKED TROUT AND WATERCRESS BAGEL

This is one of my favourite packed lunches if I know I'm going to ditch the bus and run home (hark at me showing off again!), as the carby bagel gives my muscles all the glorious glycogen they need to power me all the way!

SERVES 1

2 tablespoons low-fat cream
   cheese
½ teaspoon horseradish sauce
sprinkling of lemon zest and a
   squeeze of lemon juice
60g hot smoked trout fillet
1 small wholemeal bagel, sliced in
   half
6 slices cucumber
handful of watercress
freshly ground black pepper

Mix together the cream cheese, horseradish and lemon zest and juice in a small bowl.

Flake the fish and stir into the cream cheese mixture. Spread over one half of the bagel, top with the cucumber slices and watercress, grind over some pepper and finish with the other bagel half.

Don't be tempted to skip lunch because you want to save time and calories. You'll just end up starving and devouring half a packet of biscuits by mid afternoon. No matter how busy you are, make time for each meal.

284 CALS / **7g** FAT / **1.1g** SAT FAT / **3.8g** SUGARS / **2.15g** SALT

PRAWN MAYONNAISE

Prawn mayonnaise is the most popular sandwich filling of all time in Britain... SO COME ON GIRLS, INDULGE!

SERVES 1

1 tablespoon light mayo

½ tablespoon reduced-sugar ketchup

dash of Tabasco (optional)

dash of Worcestershire sauce (optional)

sprinkling of lemon zest and a squeeze of lemon juice

a little chopped dill, basil, coriander, parsley or tarragon – whichever you have hanging around

70g cooked peeled prawns

2 slices wholemeal bread

handful of rocket or baby spinach

freshly ground black pepper

Mix the mayo, ketchup, Tabasco and Worcestershire sauce (if using), lemon zest and juice and herbs together in a small bowl and season with black pepper.

Stir the prawns into the sauce. Pile onto one slice of bread, top with the rocket and finish the sandwich with the other slice of bread.

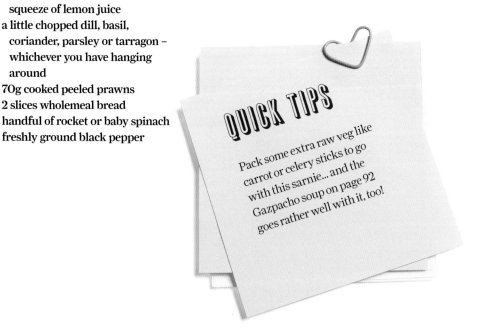

QUICK TIPS

Pack some extra raw veg like carrot or celery sticks to go with this sarnie... and the Gazpacho soup on page 92 goes rather well with it, too!

5 MINUTES

296 CALS / **4** FAT / **0.9g** SAT FAT / **6.9g** SUGARS / **2.71g** SALT

TLT
(TURKEY, LETTUCE AND TOMATO)

This is my version of the great BLT sandwich, except I make it with the much lower fat turkey rashers rather than super fatty streaky bacon. So it feels like a really naughty sarnie, but it isn't at all!

SERVES 1

4 turkey rashers
2 slices granary bread
1 tablespoon light mayo
1 medium tomato, sliced
4–5 iceberg lettuce leaves

Preheat the grill to a medium–high heat. Grill the turkey rashers until nicely crisp.

Toast the bread and then spread with the mayo. Layer the turkey rashers, tomato and lettuce over one of the slices of bread, and top with the other slice.

5 MINUTES

317 CALS / **7g** FAT / **1.9g** SAT FAT / **7.1g** SUGARS / **1.19g** SALT

BEEF, HORSERADISH AND RADISH

I can eat a beef and horseradish sandwich anytime, any place, anywhere...

SERVES 1

1 tablespoon light mayo
1 heaped teaspoon creamed
  horseradish
2 slices granary bread
handful of watercress
2 slices cold lean roast beef
4 radishes, sliced
10 cherry tomatoes

Mix the mayo and horseradish together and then spread on both your slices of bread. Now layer the watercress, beef and radishes on top and sandwich together. Munch the tomatoes with the sarnie.

*If you don't like creamed horseradish,
why not use hot English
mustard instead?*

427 CALS / **12g** FAT / **2g** SAT FAT / **5.9g** SUGARS / **1.48g** SALT

TASTE-TASTIC TURKEY

Turkey is a great low-fat sandwich filler and, of course, works beautifully with cranberry, so why not treat yourself to one of these gorgeous sarnies this lunchtime? You could even make an extra one and impress one of your friends with your generosity – just make sure you don't eat both yourself!

SERVES 1

1 tablespoon chopped walnuts
2 tablespoons light mayo
1 teaspoon finely chopped red
   onion
1 teaspoon cranberry sauce
2 slices of your favourite bread
100g lean diced or sliced turkey

Mix together all the filling ingredients (apart from the turkey) and then pile onto one slice of the bread. Then top with the turkey and sandwich together with the other slice of bread.

As with any of these sandwiches, feel free to bulk this up with a handful of your favourite salad leaves.

285 CALS / 4g FAT / 0.8g SAT FAT / 3.9g SUGARS / 2.03g SALT

CHILLI TUNA

Come on, throw that boring old tuna and cucumber sarnie in the bin and try this fantastically tarted-up version!

SERVES 1

2 tablespoons light mayo
100g tinned tuna flakes in brine, drained
5cm piece celery, finely chopped
5cm piece cucumber, chopped
pinch of chilli flakes or 1 teaspoon chopped fresh chilli
a few leaves of basil (optional, if you have some knocking about!)
2 slices granary bread
salt and freshly ground black pepper

Just mix together all the filling ingredients, season, and then sandwich together with the bread, guys!

QUICK TIPS

Lots of people don't like celery and cucumber (why?!). If you're one of these people you can swap the celery and cucumber for 1 tablespoon of tinned sweetcorn.

207 CALS / **5g** FAT / **1g** SAT FAT / **6.7g** SUGARS / **2.9g** SALT

HAM WITH HONEYED MUSTARD MAYO

Whenever I pack a sandwich (like this yummy ham and mayo delight) to take to work, I usually take a Thermos of soup, too, so I feel really full for the whole day. I also take a load of carrots to munch on too, just in case there is a skinny cow eating crisps near me! Oh, and carrots make you see in the dark, too, girls.

SERVES 1

½ teaspoon honey

1 tablespoon light mayo

1 teaspoon of your favourite
   mustard

1 wholemeal roll

3 slices lean ham (or turkey, if you
   prefer)

slices of tomato and cucumber

lettuce leaves

Mix together the honey, mayo and mustard. Open the roll and spread with the honey-mustard mayo, then pile in the ham and salad... lots of salad! It will keep you feeling full and virtuous.

If you are doing lots of exercise, add more ham or turkey as you will need the protein.

251 CALS / **14g** FAT / **2.6g** SAT FAT / **3.4g** SUGARS / **1.32g** SALT

SUPER SINFUL (TASTING) SANDWICH

Sinful tasting, but in fact not sinful at all, this sarnie is packed full with nutrient-rich, devilishly tasty ingredients.

SERVES 1

½ tablespoon light mayo
1 teaspoon of your favourite mustard
2 slices rye bread
½ small avocado, sliced
6 cherry tomatoes, sliced
handful of rocket

Mix together the mayo and mustard and spread over both slices of your rye bread. Layer the avocado and tomato slices onto one slice of the bread, then top with the rocket and the other slice of bread – job done!

You will think I am a glutton if I tell you that I sometimes add a few sneaky crisps to this sarnie... shhh!

45 **5** 15 / 0 / MINUTES / 30

207 CALS / **5g** FAT / **2.5g** SAT FAT / **4.5g** SUGARS / **1.15g** SALT

CREAM CHEESE, CUCUMBER AND WATERCRESS

A sandwich fit for a royal garden party... ever so posh, my dear!

SERVES 4

2 tablespoons low-fat cream
   cheese
2 slices half-and-half bread
1 tablespoon freshly chopped
   chives or basil (optional, if you
   have some knocking about)
handful of watercress
8 slices cucumber
salt and freshly ground black
   pepper

Spread 1 tablespoon cream cheese on each slice of bread. Layer the other ingredients onto one slice, season, then top with the other slice.

QUICK TIPS

If you don't have watercress, spinach or rocket would also work well in this fancy sandwich.

311 CALS / **8g** FAT / **1.9g** SAT FAT / **4.7g** SUGARS / **1.26g** SALT

MEXICAN MADNESS WRAP

I like to make this crazy wrap even madder by adding a lot more than a splash of chilli sauce, but you can adjust it to your own tastes.

SERVES 1

1 multi-seed tortilla wrap
50g skinless cooked cold chicken, shredded
2 tablespoons drained tinned kidney beans
1 tablespoon drained tinned sweetcorn
good splash of chilli sauce
1 tablespoon tomato salsa
handful of your favourite salad leaves
chopped fresh coriander, if you have some (optional)

Gently warm the wrap in the microwave or in a hot frying pan so it's more pliable.

Mix together all the ingredients in a bowl, pile them on to the wrap, roll and serve.

If you are veggie, swap the chicken in this wrap for half a small avocado.

334 CALS / **9g** FAT / **3.3g** SAT FAT / **13.7g** SUGARS / **1.93g** SALT

CHEESY SLAW SARNIE

I will make a confession here... this is my hangover sandwich and, as long as you don't tell anyone, I will also reveal that I sometimes do the most disgraceful thing of squishing some cheese and onion crisps into it (if it's a shocker of a hangover) and washing it down with a Diet Coke... oh and a couple of paracetamol, shhh!

SERVES 1

a matchbox size block of reduced-
   fat hard cheese, grated
1 carrot, grated
¹/₈ cabbage, grated
a little grated onion
2 slices of your fave healthy bread

For the dressing
2 tablespoons light mayo
2 teaspoons sweet vinegar
salt and freshly ground black
   pepper

Put the cheese in a bowl and then add the carrot, cabbage and onion.

Mix together the dressing ingredients in a small bowl and then stir into the grated cheese mixture.

Pile the mixture onto one slice of bread and top with the second.

If you want to reduce the fat a little here, take out the cheese and have 2 slices of lean ham with the slaw instead.

250 CALS / **17g** FAT / **3.6g** SAT FAT / **2.2g** SUGARS / **1.01g** SALT

WHO'S GOT EGG? EGG SALAD

One of the best things about being a grown up (some may argue I don't have the right to call myself that, but ho hum!) is not worrying about whether you will be an immediate social outcast if your lunch smells of egg...

SERVES 1

1 hard-boiled egg, sliced
a bowl of your favourite salad
 leaves
1 teaspoon capers
2 oatcakes or Ryvitas

For the dressing
2 teaspoons olive oil
1 teaspoon sweet vinegar (or
 whatever vinegar you want)
1 teaspoon light mayo
1 tablespoons chopped spring
 onion (the green bits)

Make the dressing by mixing together the dressing ingredients and put it in a little pot that seals well.

Wrap your crispbreads.

Put the egg, leaves and capers into a packed lunch box and ruuuuuun – the bus is there!

*I think eggs are the best thing ever
for staving off hunger.*

97 CALS / **2g** FAT / **0.3g** SAT FAT / **10.1g** SUGARS / **0.63g** SALT

THE HAPPY HUMMUS WRAP

I call this the Happy Hummus Wrap because it's bursting with goodness that will make you skip about all day... oh yeah, and it tastes pretty good, too!

SERVES 1

1 tortilla wrap
2 tablespoons homemade hummus
   (page 161)
handful of rocket, spinach or
   watercress (or all of them!)
½ raw beetroot, grated
1 carrot, grated

Gently warm the wrap in the microwave or a hot frying pan to make it more pliable. Spread the hummus over the wrap. Top with the greens, beetroot and carrot and then roll up. Wrap well enough that you don't crack into it on the bus... wait for lunch.

QUICK TIPS

You can add any veg you like to this – finely chopped celery or red pepper, maybe a little grated cucumber... the choice is yours!

265 CALS / **8g** FAT / **2.8g** SAT FAT / **4g** SUGARS / **1.81g** SALT

FANTASTIC FETA AND PEPPER

As I sit here writing, I know that I will definitely go over to the fridge any minute now and make this sandwich myself... I simply can't talk about feta, pesto and basil without wanting to eat them!

SERVES 1

2 slices of your favourite bread
   (although if your favourite bread
   is focaccia, FORGET IT!)
1 teaspoon pesto
50g flame-roasted red peppers
   from a jar, drained and finely
   chopped
30g reduced-fat feta cheese
1 teaspoon toasted pine nuts
handful of rocket (optional)

Spread the slices of bread with the pesto. Layer the other ingredients over one slice and then finish with the other slice.

Always bring your own packed lunch. Your homemade goodies will be ten times tastier than some calorie-packed, limp, pre-made sandwich – and much better for you, too!

203 CALS / **5g** FAT / **0.8g** SAT FAT / **1.2g** SUGARS / **1.32g** SALT

TASTY TUNA PASTA SALAD

I hope you use wholemeal pasta in this dish so you can feel super healthy when they're all yamming their afternoon doughnuts!

SERVES 2

200g leftover cooked pasta shapes
8 olives, pitted and sliced
2 teaspoons olive oil
squeeze of lemon juice (and some
 of the zest)
185g tin tuna in spring water,
 drained
a little chopped red onion
2 sundried tomatoes, finely
 chopped (not in oil)
a handful of basil (or whatever
 herb you fancy)

This is so simple. Just mix everything together and put into your Tupperware!

If, like my husband, you are gluten-intolerant, swap the pasta in this recipe for cooked rice.

132 CALS / **8g** FAT / **1g** SAT FAT / **7.1g** SUGARS / **0.31g** SALT
(VALUES GIVEN ARE FOR ZERO NOODLES)

NOODLES ON THE RUN

This noodle dish makes a really nice change if you have a case of sandwich-itus!

SERVES 2

400g Zero Noodles or 2 x 85g bundles buckwheat noodles
2 teaspoons sesame oil
15 mangetout
2 carrots, very thinly sliced
½ red chilli, finely chopped
20 cashew nuts or a handful of cold shredded chicken

Cook the noodles according to packet instructions. Drain, rinse under cold water and allow to drain thoroughly, then toss them in the sesame oil. Stir in the other ingredients (although I usually wrap the nuts separately and stir them in when I'm ready to eat 'cos I like 'em crunchy) and pop into your carry box.

And if you have one of those nifty soy sauce packets, take one of those along, too, and sprinkle on the top!

Zero Noodles are made from the konjac plant, and are eaten as a replacement for rice, pasta and noodles. They fill you up, but are carb-free and contain just 10 calories per pack.

187 CALS / **8g** FAT / **2.9g** SAT FAT / **4.8g** SUGARS / **1.08g** SALT

GUILT-FREE CHICKEN CAESAR SALAD

Although most of the other recipes in this section are just for one, this is a really nice salad to make up and share with a friend. And how about a cheeky little glass of white wine (or even champagne!) to go alongside it?

SERVES 2

100g cold cooked skinless chicken, shredded
iceberg lettuce, shredded
1 hard-boiled egg (optional), chopped
1 small slice brown bread
1 garlic clove, peeled
salt

For the dressing
2 tablespoons light mayo
¼ garlic clove, crushed
1 teaspoon Dijon mustard
2 teaspoons rice wine vinegar
2 tablespoons finely grated Parmesan cheese
salt and freshly ground black pepper

Put the chicken, lettuce and hard-boiled egg (if using) into a big Tupperware box.

Mix together the dressing ingredients and put into a separate pot that seals well.

Toast the bread. Rub with a cut garlic clove and sprinkle with a little salt. Cut into cubes, then wrap in a bit of tin foil and pack.

When lunchtime finally comes, simply pour the dressing over the salad, toss well and serve for you and a friend, topped with the toasted garlic bread croûtons.

Be warned – with this salad on offer, everyone will want to be your friend!

374 CALS / **23g** FAT / **8g** SAT FAT / **7.6g** SUGARS / **2.11g** SALT

BIG FAT AMERICAN SALAD

As far as I'm concerned, nobody does salad like the Americans! Huge bowls the size of the Isle of Wight, filled with an array of fabulous ingredients.

SERVES 4

2 iceberg lettuces, shredded
250g diced turkey or chicken
20 cherry tomatoes
1 ripe avocado, chopped
4 hard-boiled eggs, chopped
4 slices grilled smoked back
   bacon, fat removed, chopped

For the dressing
100ml low-fat buttermilk
3 tablespoons light mayo
1 tablespoon rice wine vinegar
70g blue cheese

For the dressing, whisk together the buttermilk, mayo and vinegar in a bowl. Crumble in the cheese and give a good stir.

Put the lettuces in a bowl with the turkey or chicken, tomatoes and avocado.

Sprinkle the eggs and bacon on top.

Drizzle over the salad dressing and you're good to go!

GREEDY GIRL GETS STRICT

Break glass in case of emergency –
for when you need an urgent detox

BREAK GLASS IN CASE OF EMERGENCY!

As someone who has been overweight for most of my adult life, there is one thing I am sure about when it comes to this whole dieting thing: fad diets do NOT work.

In fact, I think that, if anything, they eventually lead to weight gain. It's almost as if you can binge on the failure that goes hand in hand with failed dieting attempts.

This is why I realised, a long time ago, that I had in fact dieted my way to obesity. By repeatedly heading off on already doomed excursions towards weight-loss in this way or that, I found that, although I could initially stick to whatever the latest diet craze was, I would always eventually break, with the resultant binge on all the foods I'd been so cruelly denied in the first place. When I explained this to my husband, he said each diet sounded like a weird bungee jump backwards into an enormous mountain of the very same food the diet had sought to avoid in the first place! I think he is right. Whilst denial is a huge part of acknowledging whether or not one needs to lose weight in the first place, denial of a particular type of food invariably results in a full-on binge on the very same food itself!

So, every attempt I've ever made has ended up with me putting back on any weight I'd lost, plus a cheeky bit more just to make me feel a little more ghastly about myself each time. It's just plain bonkers to ask anyone to go without carbs, sugar or alcohol for any length of time (especially someone like me, who'd hand over her own children in exchange for carbs, sugar and alcohol) without expecting a binge at the end of it!

Nope, I'm a great believer in the idea of having a little of what you fancy in order to stay on the straight and narrow slim girls' path. It's also important to remember that it actually takes a hell of a long time to pile on the pounds, so, whether we like it or not, we need to give ourselves a bit of time to take them off. If

But what do we do when we don't want to do the sensible thing and take time to lose weight, just as we took an awful lot of time gaining it?

we do, we will have a far better chance of actually keeping them off!!

But what do we do when we don't want to do the sensible thing and take time to lose weight, just as we took an awful lot of time gaining it?! After all, emergencies do arise where we need to shift a couple of pounds and we need to shift them fast!

Now, of course, we all know the 'blah blah' scientific facts about how, if you lose weight very quickly, it's fat fraud, and most of it's going to be excess fluid and not fat!

But if it's 'excess', and losing it is going to get us into that little black dress by Saturday, or de-bloat our stomachs just enough for that swimsuit that we just have to wear at the weekend... well, I'm sorry, but it's 'See you later excess fluid!'.

It's just good old-fashioned unreasonable to say we can never take extreme measures when we are in dire need. Whether we are supposed to or not, let's face it – we always will!

So, with that in mind, I've devised this 'Break Glass in Case of Emergency' three-day plan, which is very low in calories, but high in nutrients, so you don't end up feeling half-dead and looking like a zombie!

Stick to it rigidly and you will shift anything from two to six pounds (1–3kg), depending on how much weight you have to lose. Make sure you don't stay on the plan for longer than three days, though, or your body will go into starvation mode and will hang on for dear life to all that nasty fat which, of course, will get you right back into that vicious cycle again!

Anyway, my lovelies, here are the dos and don'ts for the next three days!

1 Try not to use any extra salt. Yuck, I know, but it will help you shift that dreaded excess fluid that's stopping that zip from going all the way up!

2 Drink plenty of water but (boo hoo) no alcohol, milk, fruit juice or sugared drinks.

3 Keep busy. If you sit around thinking about what you can't eat eventually you will just end up eating it! Distract yourself.

4 Don't eat any extra fruit, but stick to the vegetable quota to make sure you're getting enough vitamins.

5 Don't be afraid to exercise – it won't kill you! Always opt for movement rather than anything that assists you (don't drive – walk; don't take escalators or lifts, just stairs).

6 Only eat what is on the plan. If you start substituting things, it will be just the start of a very slippery sloped decline.

7 Have a cup of my Power Soup with meals when indicated. It's nourishing and will keep the hunger pangs at bay!

45 / 0 / 15 / 30 **20** MINUTES

66 CALS / **2g** FAT / **0.3g** SAT FAT / **5g** SUGARS / **0.6g** SALT

POWER SOUP

I call this my Power Soup because it literally blasts my hunger away and gives me the power to get through the day without breaking my resolve.

MAKES 10 SERVINGS

1 tablespoon olive oil
2 medium onions, chopped
2 garlic cloves, chopped
head of celery
whole head of broccoli, stalk chopped, and head broken into florets
small pointed cabbage, chopped
1 stock cube, crumbled
two mugfuls of petits pois

Heat the oil in a large saucepan over a low-medium heat. Add the onions, garlic and celery and gently cook until softened but NOT browned.

Throw in the chopped broccoli stalks and cook for a few minutes, then add the broccoli florets and cabbage.

Add 2 litres boiling water, crumble in the stock cube and cook for 5 minutes, then add the petits pois and cook until they are just tender.

Blitz in a blender, adding more stock if you prefer a thinner soup.

QUICK TIPS

You can, of course, swap any of the vegetables here for whatever veggies you prefer.

DAY ONE

BREAKFAST 101 CALS / 7g FAT / 1.9g SAT FAT / 0.4g SUGARS / 0.48g SALT

POACHED EGG & SPINACH

glass of hot water and lemon
1 egg
handful of spinach
cup of herbal tea, black coffee or
  whatever tea keeps you sane

Whilst you're drinking your hot water and lemon, poach the egg according to the method on page 30. Steam your spinach and serve, topped with the egg.

LUNCH 106 CALS / 5g FAT / 0.8g SAT FAT / 5.1g SUGARS / 0.6g SALT

SOUP & SEEDS

1 teaspoon pumpkin seeds
1 teaspoon sunflower seeds
large bowl of Power Soup
  (see page 123)

Simply sprinkle the seeds on to the soup.

DINNER 224 CALS / 3g FAT / 0.4g SAT FAT / 3.8g SUGARS / 0.56g SALT

STEAMED FISH & BROCCOLI

200g white fish
6 broccoli florets
zest of ½ lemon
1 cup of Power Soup
  (see page 123)

Steam the fish until cooked through, about 4–5 minutes. Steam the broccoli until tender, 3–4 minutes. Serve, topped with the lemon zest, with the Power Soup on the side.

DAY TWO

170 CALS / 5g FAT / 0.5g SAT FAT / 19g SUGARS / 0.37g SALT

BANANA, BERRY & VANILLA SMOOTHIE

¼ banana
100g frozen berries
240ml soya or skimmed milk
½ teaspoon vanilla extract
1 tablespoon soya protein powder

Blitz all the ingredients together
and drink!

LUNCH 105 CALS / 6g FAT / 1.5g SAT FAT / 2.4g SUGARS / 0.18g SALT

BOILED EGG & ASPARAGUS SOLDIERS

5 asparagus spears
1 egg
freshly ground black pepper

Steam the asparagus for 2–4 minutes until tender. Boil
the egg for 3 minutes until it's just soft.
Serve with the asparagus soldiers and lots of black
pepper.

DINNER 372 CALS / 8g FAT / 1.2g SAT FAT / 16.7g SUGARS / 1.69g SALT

TUNA SALAD

a little chopped red onion (optional)
6 basil leaves

185g tin tuna in spring water,
  drained
4 black olives
1 tomato, cubed
2 carrots, chopped
large handful of rocket
handful of baby spinach
4 small new potatoes, boiled
  and cooled

For the dressing
1 teaspoon lemon juice
1 teaspoon rice wine vinegar
1 teaspoon olive oil
freshly ground black pepper

Place the salad ingredients into a large bowl and mix.

Mix together the dressing ingredients and drizzle over
the salad. Serve with a cup of Power Soup (page 123).

DAY THREE

BREAKFAST · 95 CALS / 3g FAT / 0.3g SAT FAT / 15g SUGARS / 0.01g SALT

APPLE & ALMONDS

1 medium apple
5 almonds

Just munch together!

LUNCH · 199 CALS / 9g FAT / 1.7g SAT FAT / 3.5g SUGARS / 2.37g SALT

SMOKED TROUT SALAD

60g watercress
¼ cucumber, sliced
100g smoked trout (or cooked
   skinless chicken breast)
1 teaspoon lemon juice
1 teaspoon rice wine vinegar
1 teaspoon olive oil
1 cup of Power Soup (see page 123)

Put the watercress and cucumber in a bowl and flake the smoked trout on top.

Mix together the lemon, vinegar and oil and drizzle over the salad. Serve with the soup on the side.

DINNER · 279 CALS / 5g FAT / 1.2g SAT FAT / 6.2g SUGARS / 0.58g SALT

CHICKEN, COURGETTE & QUINOA SALAD

1 x 165g skinless chicken breast
juice of 1 lime
1 teaspoon pesto
1 courgette, diced
1 tomato, diced
2 tablespoons cooked quinoa
a little chopped fresh mint and
   flat-leaf parsley

Make three shallow slashes in the chicken breast and then rub the lime juice and pesto into them. Grill the chicken under a medium heat for about 3–4 minutes on each side until cooked through – but don't overcook it and dry it out! Meanwhile, steam the courgette for 2–3 minutes until just tender.

Stir the courgette and diced tomato into the quinoa with the chopped herbs. Lay the chicken on top and you're ready to eat!

NEEDY GREEDY GIRLS

Beat temptation with these naughty-but-nice 'junk food' options

THE GOOD, THE BAD AND THE UGLY

You know the feeling. You wake up and you're immediately aware of a dark shadow passing over your soul. It's as though someone crept in overnight and turned off all the lights, throwing your mind and heart into a foggy cesspit of spiralling self-hatred and depression.

It might be the early manouevres of a low-flying hangover; the distant throb of an imminent premenstrual tsunami; the slow-dawning, bleary-eyed realisation that whilst yesterday you woke up as a couple, today you're singularly single; perhaps it's even the fact that as you come to and open your eyes, the downpour outside matches a downpour in your heart about where on earth you're heading in life, love and work.

You know the days. The days you inexplicably need a hug. You need a shoulder to cry on. You need an excuse to punch your fella in the face. You need vast amounts of gifts bought immediately. You need to be invited to a glamorous party held in your honour.

You need HELP! Emotional help... And you need it NOW!

Of course none of these materialise – well, bar the punching of the fella in the face – and so we enter the everyday spiral of feeling needy, which basically translates into meaning one simple, damaging thing. We are now Needy AND Greedy! Two states of mind designed to do just one thing effectively: sabotage our diets.

Put simply, when we're Needy, we're Greedy in a way we've never known before. We're Greedy in a greedy way that knows no bounds. 'Needy Greedy' makes plain old Greedy look like a walk in the park (with a sausage roll in your mouth). 'Needy Greedy' is a condition that means (around food) we are a little like something from *The Exorcist* – spinning head, insane gabbling, eyes on stalks, arms tethered to the bed head – as you fight against the desire to scramble and hunt for every single little junk food morsel known to man (and woman!).

Put simply, when we're needy, we're greedy in a way we've never known before. We're greedy in a greedy way that knows no bounds.

For some reason the mental arithmetic runs something like this:

I feel so emotionally bereft and at sea that I am little more than a piece of junk – therefore I will do something that mirrors this: EAT JUNK.

Junk in mind + junk in heart = junk in stomach.

But what's wrong with a bit of junk now and then? After all, we're never going to get rid of those days when we wake up wanting to kill ourselves and everyone close to us for no good reason. We won't ever remove, completely, the desire to cram ourselves with rubbishy, disposable food just to plug that horrid feeling of neediness.

Well, that's why I've devised these quick recipes. They're hand grenades of tasty sustenance in times of explosive need. They're snack solutions that will deliver just a little of the junk fix we all crave, but that are actually kinder to our bodies – so that when we come out the other side of feeling Needy and Greedy, we aren't any bigger and, as a result, even Needier and Greedier than ever.

I give you the good, the bad, the ugly – good for you junk food.

Best of all, most of these no junk, junk food snacks are ready to munch in just 5 minutes or less!

UNDER **5** MINUTES
45 15 30 0

410 CALS / **15g** FAT / **2.1g** SAT FAT / **6.4g** SUGARS / **2.63g** SALT

FISH FINGER BUTTY

Sometimes if there is a jar of tartare sauce hanging about in the fridge, I use it instead of the ketchup and mayo – your choice!

SERVES 1

4 fish fingers
2 slices of half-and-half bread
1 tablespoon ketchup
1 tablespoon light mayo
watercress or salad leaves

Simply grill the fish fingers under a medium heat for 2–3 minutes on each side and slather the bread with the ketchup and mayo. Top with the watercress or salad leaves and sandwich together. Sometimes I can't resist popping a few chips (page 145) in mine!

UNDER **5** MINUTES
45 15 30 0

368 CALS / **21g** FAT / **4.4g** SAT FAT / **2.6g** SUGARS / **1.32g** SALT

AVOCADO AND MARMITE TOAST

However weird you think I am for suggesting this, please try it anyway!

SERVES 1

2 slices wholegrain bread
Marmite
1 small, ripe avocado, peeled and sliced

Toast your bread, spread it with a little Marmite, and then layer the avocado slices on top.

UNDER **5** MINUTES
45 0 15
30

350 CALS / **9g** FAT / **3.3g** SAT FAT / **24.9g** SUGARS / **6.07g** SALT

CHEESY SOUP

I have to say I am rather proud of this one...

SERVES 1

1 small tin low-calorie cream of
   tomato soup
1 or 2 small slices of bread
30g reduced-fat Cheddar or other
   hard cheese, grated
dash of Tabasco sauce

Whilst you heat up your soup, toast the bread on one side, then turn it over and and sprinkle the cheese on top. Grill till it's just bubbling.

Stir the Tabasco into the soup and then either float the cheesy toast on top or serve it alongside.

QUICK TIPS

Sometimes we all need to indulge in a little comfort food – but it's easy to trim off the calories and still have the comfort without the guilt.

45 **5** 15
MINUTES
0 30

373 CALS / **13g** FAT / **3.6g** SAT FAT / **2.9g** SUGARS / **1.46g** SALT

TUNA CHEESE MELT

Cheese and tuna? I know, soo strange – but it does work, I promise!

SERVES 2

200g tinned tuna in spring water, drained

3 spring onions, finely chopped (or any onion you have)

3 tablespoons light mayo

4 slices granary bread

50g reduced-fat Cheddar or other hard cheese, grated

salt and freshly ground black pepper

Heat the grill until it's nice and hot. Flake the tuna into a bowl and mix in the spring onions and mayo. Add some salt and freshly ground black pepper.

Toast the bread under the grill on both sides, then spread the tuna mixture on top, right to the edges of the toast. Scatter over the cheese and put back under the grill until the cheese is bubbling.

Lots of sliced tomatoes and a little sea salt will help ease the pain.

Serve a big bowl of salad on the side and this turns from a quick and easy comfort fix into a proper meal.

UNDER **5** MINUTES
0 15 30 45

366 CALS / **10g** FAT / **2g** SAT FAT / **27.4g** SUGARS / **0.5g** SALT

PEANUT BUTTER AND BANANA TOASTIE

Sticky and sweet, but healthy too...

SERVES 1

2 slices granary bread
1 banana, peeled and sliced
1 teaspoon honey
1 tablespoon peanut butter

Toast your bread. Meanwhile, mash the banana with the honey using a fork. Spread on one of the pieces of toast, then spread the peanut butter on the other one and sandwich together.

QUICK TIPS

Bananas are high in potassium, which helps to relieve hangovers. So if you're suffering the after effects of indulging too much the night before, this little treat could help to sort you out.

10 MINUTES 45 0 15 30

357 CALS / 13g FAT / 4.4g SAT FAT / 5g SUGARS / 3.06g SALT

BACON AND EGG MUFFIN

Hungover? Well, here you go...

SERVES 1

1 medium egg
2 rashers back bacon, fat removed (well, maybe leave a bit on!)
1 tomato, sliced
1 slice reduced-fat Cheddar or other hard cheese
1 super-soft muffin
salt and freshly ground black pepper

Boil the egg for 8 minutes. Once it's cool enough to handle, peel and slice.

Meanwhile, grill the bacon until nice and crisp.

Pile the tomato, cheese, bacon and egg into your muffin. Season to taste and serve.

QUICK TIPS

If your head isn't too bad and you can bear to wait a few extra minutes, arrange this sandwich with the cheese on top, pop under the grill until the cheese is bubbling and then serve!

109 CALS / **2g** FAT / **0.3g** SAT FAT / **5.3g** SUGARS / **0.47g** SALT
(PER 100G)

CHIPS AND SAUCES

Sometimes in life, only chips will do...

loads of potatoes, peeled
spray olive oil
sea salt
ketchup, light mayo, curry sauce
(weirdos), chilli sauce – whatever
it takes to hit the spot

Preheat the oven to 200°C/Gas 6.

Cut the potatoes into chips. Lay them out on a baking tray and spray well with the oil. Sprinkle with sea salt and pop in the oven for 25 minutes, turning half way through.

Serve in a big bowl with your fave dips!

42 CALS / **0g** FAT / **0g** SAT FAT / **6.3g** SUGARS / **0.55g** SALT
(PER CARROT)

CARROTS DIPPED IN MARMITE

This might sound really weird to some, but might just hit the spot for others...

carrots, peeled
Marmite

Simply dip raw carrots in Marmite and munch!

240 CALS / **12g** FAT / **6.8g** SAT FAT / **32.1g** SUGARS / **0.02g** SALT

STRAWBERRIES AND CHOCOLATE

Good riddance to him...

SERVES 1

6 cubes of dark chocolate
8–10 strawberries

Put the chocolate in a heatproof, non-metallic bowl. Place in the microwave and heat in short 20-second blasts, stirring in between, until melted.

Lie on the sofa. Dip the strawberries in the melted chocolate and enjoy...

AND BETTER STILL!

Hoorah! Good news! It's a scientific fact – chocolate is good for you!

UNDER **5** MINUTES
0 15 30 45

220 CALS / **4g** FAT / **1.6g** SAT FAT / **8g** SUGARS / **2.22g** SALT

CRUMPETS AND ICE CREAM

Really... yes, you can...

SERVES 2

2 crumpets
3 tablespoons low-fat ice cream
1 tablespoon shop-bought
chocolate sauce

Toast the crumpets, top with the ice cream and chocolate sauce, and the world will seem a better place.

As long as you keep active and make sure you get plenty of fruit and veg, it's fine – more than fine – to enjoy a few sweet treats every now and again. In fact, I believe it helps you to stay on track!

BLOODY MARY

I slipped this in without my publishers seeing (they would not approve)... sometimes only the hair of the dog will do.

SERVES 1

25ml vodka
large glass of tomato juice
good splash of Worcestershire
    sauce
squeeze of lemon juice
splash of Tabasco
1–2 celery sticks

Simply mix together and serve in a chilled glass with a stick or two of celery...

QUICK TIPS

I strongly recommend that you stick to just one of these hairy dogs!

98 CALS / **1.8g** FAT / **0.7g** SAT FAT / **12g** SUGARS / **0.16g** SALT

NOT-SO-NAUGHTY FAIRIES

Now, what would life be without cake o'clock?! Any diet that bans cake must be kicked to the kerb!

SERVES 12

110g caster sugar
2 eggs, whisked
110g self-raising flour
1 teaspoon vanilla extract

For the frosting
3 tablespoons low-fat cream
  cheese
2 tablespoons good-quality cocoa
  powder
2 tablespoons icing sugar

To serve
12 strawberries

Preheat the oven to 190°C/Gas 5 and line a 12-hole fairy cake tin with paper cases.

Now this is all very easy, because all you have to do is put all the ingredients in a bowl and beat together, then spoon the batter into the paper cases. Bake for 15–18 minutes until risen, then remove them from the tin and allow to cool completely.

To make the frosting, beat together all the frosting ingredients until smooth. Then pipe onto the fairy cakes and top with the strawberries. Cake o'clock, everyone!!

QUICK TIPS

Because these little beauties don't contain butter, they're low in fat – but the flipside is they won't last as long as regular fairy cakes. They're so delicious, they won't last long anyway – just make sure you have some friends to help!

MY TAKE ON THE TAKEAWAY

Your favourite takeaway treats without the extra calories – and just as fast!

MY TAKE ON THE TAKEAWAY

Have you ever noticed how, when you're really hungry, and you're on a diet, some smart arse always seems to shout, with wild abandon, 'Anyone fancy a takeaway?!'

What kind of a question is that?! Of course *I* fancy a takeaway! Of course *you* fancy a takeaway! Who doesn't? I mean, after all, we're all Greedy Girls (and boys), aren't we?

'YES! Of course I fancy a bloody takeaway!' you yell back. 'BUT I'M ON A DIET, YOU KNUCKLE BRAIN!'

So, what should you do when this irritating scenario plays out for the zillionth time and you feel your reserve and willpower draining away by the second?

Well, this is probably the moment you should call on me, the Greedy Girl! The hostess-with-the-mostess who can generally find a way to indulge you where other dieters have repeatedly failed.

This doesn't mean I'm going to suggest you call your local takeaway

(step away from the phone!) and order something naughty that you can then wave a magical takeaway wand over to somehow make it calorie friendly.

No. But I am going to help you to indulge in the flavours, the excitement, the expectation and the greedy indulgence of what it means to tuck into your very own takeaway.

We all know we want to be slim and healthy! But we also all know that, where we can, we want it all! Deprivation simply isn't our 'thang!' I mean, a life without the joys of sweet and sour pork, fried rice, spicy kebabs, curries and jerk chicken is not, quite frankly, a life really worth living.

Okay, I know I'm prone to being a bit of a drama queen about these things, but – put simply – I'm just not prepared to put up with it! Are you?!

A life without takeaway? If that's what dieting is about, you may as well take ME away – in a white van!

Okay – rant over! I must apologise! ... But, hang on – why should I?! (Sorry,

You won't feel deprived if you feast on these recipes next time you fancy a takeaway.

I'm off again!)

I DO have rage about this! In fact, I have brown paper bags and tinfoil cartons FULL of greedy rage charging around London right now on the back of scooters as they scuttle around the streets, delivering temptation to every doorstep!

When I think about just how much food there is on offer to us all – everywhere, 24/7 – that we simply have to avoid eating in order to avoid imminent obesity, it makes me furious. Going about one's daily activities is like a snacking equivalent of the Grand National, with enormous hurdles presented before you at every turn! Not only, as I've mentioned before, are there vending machines breeding all over the nation, but there are now more and more mopeds and scooters hurtling around the country, quite literally delivering our increased waistlines to our very own front doors!

Deep breath!

Okay. I think I've finally got a handle on this ... I'm now going to turn this into a positive! Forget the takeaway knock at the FRONT door. This next section is about all the Greedy Girl Takeaway dishes that I'm now going to let you sneak in through the BACK door!

Yep, I've created a whole host of Greedy Girl-friendly takeaway meals, the ingredients for which I've slashed away at, with my trusted calorie sword, in order to get rid of thousands of calories! I've dispensed with the ghee, the chicken skin and fatty meats! I've flushed the double cream and butter down the sink, kissing goodbye to thousands of calories in the process.

BUT, I promise you, assure you, and wholeheartedly guarantee that you won't feel deprived if you feast on the recipes here next time you're desperate for the evils of a takeaway.

Not only will you love every mouthful, but at the end you won't feel like an over-stuffed naan bread for the rest of the evening! Not bad, eh?!

408 CALS / 13g FAT / 2.8g SAT FAT / 34.7g SUGARS / 2.69g SALT

SWEET AND SOUR PORK

This has less than half the calories the same one would have in my local Chinese, but is still sticky, sweet and a little sour, too. I've managed this by not committing the dastardly act of battering and deep-frying the pork! And, personally, I think it tastes all the better!

SERVES 4

4 pork loin chops, fat removed,
   cut into 2cm cubes
2 garlic cloves, peeled and chopped
4cm piece fresh ginger, peeled and
   finely grated
2 tablespoons vegetable oil
1 medium onion, cut into eighths
2 each of red, green and yellow
   peppers, deseeded and sliced
100g beansprouts
350g tin pineapple chunks in
   juice (drain and reserve the juice)
green parts of 3 spring onions,
   finely sliced
sea salt and freshly ground black
   pepper

For the sauce:
2 heaped teaspoons cornflour
100ml chicken stock (made with a
   stock cube)
150ml reserved pineapple juice
   (see above)
3 tablespoons dark soy sauce
2 tablespoons soft brown sugar
2 tablespoons tomato ketchup
1 teaspoon chilli paste (optional)
2 teaspoons rice wine vinegar

Put the pork in a small bowl with the garlic and ginger, mix, and set aside.

To make the sauce, put the cornflour into a bowl, add 2 tablespoons of the stock and mix together to make a smooth paste. Now pour the pineapple juice, soy sauce, sugar, ketchup, chilli paste (if using) and rice wine vinegar and the rest of the stock into the cornflour paste. Give it all a good stir and set aside.

Heat a wok over a high heat and add 1 tablespoon of the oil. Once the oil is really hot, throw in the cubed pork with the ginger and garlic and stir-fry in two batches until it is nicely sealed and slightly golden. Remove and set aside.

Pour the remaining tablespoon of oil into the wok. Add the onion and peppers and stir-fry for a couple of minutes.

Now put the pork back into the wok and stir-fry again for a minute or so. Give your sweet and sour sauce a good stir and then pour over the pork and veg.

Taste and season if needed. Reduce the heat and cook gently until the pork is cooked through. A couple of minutes before the end, throw in the beansprouts, pineapple chunks and sliced spring onions.

Serve with either Zero Noodles or a small cup of cooked rice per person.

309 CALS / **10g** FAT / **1.7g** SAT FAT / **17.1g** SUGARS / **3.77g** SALT
(VALUES GIVEN FOR ZERO NOODLES VERSION)

CHICKEN CHOW MEIN

If you're vegetarian, why not replace the chicken with smoked tofu or cashew nuts and extra veg... in fact, even if you aren't a vegetarian, why not add some extra veg? The more veg, the better!

SERVES 4

400g skinless chicken breast, sliced into strips

2 teaspoons five-spice powder

2 tablespoons groundnut oil (this is best, but you can use any vegetable oil)

2cm piece fresh ginger, peeled and grated

3 medium carrots, thinly sliced

250g water chestnuts, drained and halved

800g Zero Noodles or 400g dried rice noodles

6 spring onions, sliced

2 tablespoons chopped cashew nuts

salt and freshly ground black pepper

For the sauce

2 tablespoons soft light brown sugar

2 tablespoons cornflour

4 tablespoons dark soy sauce

3 tablespoons dry sherry

75ml chicken stock (made with a stock cube)

Put the chicken in a bowl and sprinkle with the five-spice powder. Season with salt and pepper and mix well.

Now make the sauce. In a separate small bowl, mix the sugar and cornflour together with the soy sauce, sherry and chicken stock, mixing until you have a smooth paste. Set aside.

Heat 1 tablespoon of the oil in a large, non-stick frying pan, and then, once it's really hot, fry the chicken in two batches. (Doing it in two batches is important because you want to make sure it fries rather than steams.) Remove the chicken to a plate and set aside.

Heat the remaining oil in the wok and fry the ginger, carrots and water chestnuts over a high heat for a minute or two.

Cook the noodles according to the packet instructions, and, while they are cooking, add the spring onions and chicken to the wok and pour the sauce over. Cook for a couple of minutes until the chicken is cooked through (but don't overcook it, or the chicken will become tough).

Drain the 'wonder' noodles and add to the other ingredients in the wok. Give it all a good stir. Divide the chow mein between four bowls and sprinkle the chopped cashew nuts on top of each one. Now you can 'chow' down.

221 CALS / **2g** FAT / **0.7g** SAT FAT / **9.6g** SUGARS / **0.25g** SALT

CHICKEN SHISH KEBAB

I always say that if you are out late at night and are hit with a raging hunger, a shish kebab is the absolute best takeaway to go for! It's basically grilled chicken, veg and salad (saintly!), served in a warmed pitta bread (make it a wholemeal one for extra brownie points). Perfect! And, as long as you don't have a side of chips, and a rum baba for pud, you'll be a bit of an angel! But for those of you who aren't stumbling home from the pub, and just really fancy a super-tasty, healthy, satisfying kebab, here's the perfect recipe.

SERVES 4

4 skinless, boneless chicken
  breasts, cut into bite-sized pieces
1 each of green, red and yellow
  peppers, chopped into chunks
2 medium red onions, cut into
  bite-sized pieces
20 button mushrooms, kept whole
2 garlic cloves, finely chopped
½ teaspoon ground cumin
½ teaspoon cayenne pepper
½ teaspoon ground black pepper
juice of 1 lemon
good pinch of salt

Mix together all the ingredients in a large bowl. If your lemon turns out to not be very juicy, add more to taste.

When you're ready to cook your guilt-free kebabs, simply thread the marinated chicken and vegetable pieces onto skewers (if you're using wooden ones, don't forget to soak them well first) and then cook either on a hot barbecue, under a hot grill, or indeed, you guessed it, on a hot griddle until the chicken is cooked through.

Serve with a big salad and a pitta bread or tortilla wrap for each person.

HUMMUS

You don't even want to know how fattening most shop bought hummus is. This is because it is loaded with oil and lots of tahini, so I have taken all the oil out and some of the tahini and swiftly shaved hundreds of calories off the finished dish! Clever me... by the way, it's still delicious, of course!

SERVES 4

400g tin chickpeas
2 tablespoons tahini
3 tablespoons lemon juice
1 teaspoon salt
1 garlic clove, minced

To garnish
paprika
chopped fresh flat-leaf parsley

Tip the chickpeas and their liquid into a saucepan and warm through, then drain – but don't pour the liquid down the sink, you'll need it later!

Tip the chickpeas, together with all the other ingredients, into a blender and blend together. If the mixture seems too thick, add a little of the reserved liquid. You will need to taste – it might need more lemon (it usually does) or a bit more salt. You can either have it quite chunky or super smooth – whatever makes you happy!

Now spoon the hummus into a serving bowl, make a hollow in the centre with the back of a dessertspoon, sprinkle a little paprika round the edge, and drop the chopped parsley into the middle.

Serve with kebabs and salad.

You could serve this as a starter with cubes of grilled lamb on top – yum!

142 CALS / **6g** FAT / **2.4g** SAT FAT / **0.5g** SUGARS / **0.13g** SALT

A PROPER DONER KEBAB

I don't think any of us want to even think about what is actually in a doner kebab from a kebab shop, or admit we have ever eaten one! But we all know we have, and most of us have probably loved it! Well, there is nothing shameful about the recipe below, but it is bloomin' lovely.

SERVES 4

For the lamb

400g leg of lamb, trimmed of fat, cut into really thin strips

2 tablespoons cider vinegar

juice of 1 juicy lemon

1 teaspoon grated lemon zest

1 teaspoon cinnamon

1 teaspoon allspice

1 teaspoon each of salt and freshly ground black pepper

½ teaspoon ground cardamom

1 small onion, grated

1 small tomato, grated

1 tablespoon finely chopped fresh flat-leaf parsley

To serve

½ cucumber, sliced

2 medium tomatoes, sliced

1 red onion, finely sliced

sprinkle of freshly chopped mint (optional)

a squeeze of lemon juice

4 pitta breads or tortillas

salt

Put all the ingredients for the lamb in a bowl and leave to marinate until you are ready to cook (this could be anything from 10 minutes to 48 hours!).

When you're ready to eat, put the salad vegetables (and if you're using it, the chopped mint) onto a plate. Squeeze over some lemon and sprinkle with salt. Put the marinated lamb in a sieve to drain thoroughly.

The marinated meat is gorgeous cooked on a barbie, but if not, put it under a very hot grill. Whichever way you choose, it will only take minutes before it's ready! Turn during cooking so it cooks through evenly.

Heat the pitta breads or tortillas either in a microwave or, as I do, in a dry frying pan. Divide the grilled meat between them, load it up with the minty salad and it's time for your takeaway!

222 CALS / **2g** FAT / **0.7g** SAT FAT / **5.8g** SUGARS / **2.25g** SALT

JERK CHICKEN

Yuuuuummmmyyyy! I love jerk chicken and I can't quite believe I only tried it for the first time a few months ago! Decades of time gone, taken, lost without jerk chicken in my life! Madness that I'm not sure I will ever get over! You can use this marinade on any meat or fish you like, and, of course, throw in some more of those dastardly Scotch bonnet chillies if you want smoke coming out of your eyes!

SERVES 4

4 tablespoons lime juice or cider vinegar
2 teaspoons dried thyme
2 tablespoons brown sugar
2 teaspoons ground allspice
2 teaspoons ground cinnamon
2 teaspoons ground ginger
1 teaspoon smoked paprika
2 teaspoons ground nutmeg
1 teaspoon salt
1 teaspoon ground black pepper
8 garlic cloves, finely chopped
1 medium onion, quartered
4 tablespoons soy sauce
2 Scotch bonnet peppers (or, if you prefer it a bit milder, jalapeño), finely sliced
4 large skinless chicken breasts

Put all the ingredients apart from the chicken into a processor and joodge until smooth. Then rub this violently hot marinade into the chicken and leave to marinate (for as long as you've got). Remember to wash your hands thoroughly afterwards.

This would usually be cooked on the barbie to get that authentic, charred taste, but you can cook it under the grill or on a griddle pan at a medium heat. The chicken shouldn't take long to cook, just a few minutes each side – just make sure each breast is cooked through, but not overcooked. Serve with rice and peas (see page 166).

20 MINUTES

380 CALS / **10g** FAT / **7.7g** SAT FAT / **3.9g** SUGARS / **0.71g** SALT

RICE AND PEAS

You CANNOT have jerk chicken without rice and peas! You just cannot! Need I say more?

SERVES 4

400g tin light coconut milk
400g tin black-eyed beans (or
  kidney beans), drained
1 teaspoon coconut or vegetable oil
1 medium onion, grated
250g basmati rice
1 teaspoon dried thyme
2 garlic cloves, chopped
vegetable stock (optional)
1 whole red chilli
salt and freshly ground black
  pepper

Pour the coconut milk into a jug, then add the drained beans.

Heat the oil in a large saucepan over a low heat. Gently fry the grated onion in the oil until it begins to soften, then tip in the rice, thyme and garlic, and stir for a minute.

Pour in the coconut milk and beans, and, if necessary, top up with boiling water or stock to come about 2cm above the top of the rice. Add salt if you think it needs it – if you have used stock it might be salty enough. Bring to the boil and boil for 1 minute. Lower the heat, place the whole chilli on top of the rice, cover the pan tightly and simmer for about 15 minutes, or until holes begin to appear on top of the rice and the rice is tender.

Serve with the Jerk Chicken (page 164) and a salad.

467 CALS / **10g** FAT / **3.6g** SAT FAT / **25g** SUGARS / **1.04g** SALT

CHICKEN ROTI ROLL-UPS

These are a great Saturday-night-in-front-of-a-movie treat! But they are also always a huge success on any picnic too. You could, of course, double up the ingredients and have some as a packed lunch.

SERVES 4

1 tablespoon coconut or
   vegetable oil
1 medium onion, grated
4 garlic cloves, grated
1 Scotch bonnet pepper (if you're
   crazy for the heat), deseeded and
   chopped
2 tablespoons curry powder
4 skinless, boneless chicken
   breasts, sliced thinly lengthways
100ml chicken stock
4 large tortilla wraps

For a cheeky little salsa
2 large ripe mangoes, peeled and
   cubed
½ cucumber, cubed
juice of 1 lime
½ teaspoon honey
2 tablespoons chopped fresh
   coriander
a little chopped red chilli
   (optional)

Heat the oil in a non-stick frying pan over a medium heat. Add the onion, garlic and Scotch bonnet pepper and fry until soft. Stir in the curry powder and fry for about a minute.

Stir in the chicken pieces and fry for a couple of minutes. Pour in the chicken stock, bring to the bubble and cook, uncovered, for a couple of minutes until the chicken is cooked through.

Meanwhile, make the salsa. Simply put all the ingredients into a bowl and give it a good stir.

To serve, heat the tortillas in the microwave or in a dry frying pan until they are nice and soft, then spoon the chicken curry equally between them. Now roll them up and cut each one into two. Serve with the cheeky salsa.

181 CALS / **9g** FAT / **5.8g** SAT FAT / **3g** SUGARS / **1.06g** SALT

PRAWN CURRY IN A HURRY

Prawn Curry in a Hurry could easily be in the 10-minute section of this book as it is so quick to make, but I knew there would be a risk of letters of complaint coming in as the rice would hold things up a wee bit!

SERVES 4

2 tablespoons Madras curry paste
pinch of sugar
300ml light coconut milk
400g raw, peeled prawns
100g mangetout
1 tablespoon Brinjal pickle
fresh coriander to garnish,
   chopped
1 small cup plain boiled rice per
   person, to serve

Heat up a wok and fry the curry paste for a minute or two, stirring the whole time.

Add a pinch of sugar, give it another stir and then pour in your coconut milk. Let it bubble away for a few minutes until the sauce thickens.

Throw in the prawns and mangetout, reduce the heat and cook for a couple of minutes until the prawns go just pink. Don't overcook them, as they will become tough – yuck!

Stir in the Brinjal pickle, garnish with chopped coriander and serve with the rice.

283 CALS / **9g** FAT / **4.1g** SAT FAT / **8.3g** SUGARS / **0.68g** SALT

CHICKEN JALFREZI

Jalfrezi is my husband's favourite curry from our local curry house. It is delicious, BUT they use a loooot of oil, and I've estimated that the dish alone, even without rice or naan bread, comes to about 700 calories. So I've reduced massively (though not completely, 'cos that would just be dull) the amount of oil used, but it's lost none of its flavour as it's packed with plenty of onion, garlic, spices and vegetables. Mmmm.

SERVES 4

1 tablespoon coconut/vegetable oil
2 medium onions, cut into eighths
6 garlic cloves, 2 of them finely
  chopped, 4 quartered
1–6 green chillies, finely chopped
  (depending on how much of your
  head you want to blow off!)
3cm piece fresh ginger, grated
1 red and 1 green pepper, deseeded
  and sliced (optional)
5 large skinless, boneless chicken
  breasts, visible fat removed, cut
  into 4cm chunks
1 tablespoon ground cumin
1 tablespoon ground coriander
1 teaspoon turmeric
400g tin plum tomatoes
large pinch of sugar
100ml chicken stock
pinch of garam masala
1 tablespoon cornflour

To garnish
2 tablespoons low-fat Greek
  yogurt
chopped fresh coriander, to taste
1 teaspoon dry-fried nigella seeds
  (optional)

Heat the oil over a medium-high heat in a large, non-stick frying pan. Throw in the onions, all the garlic, chilli, ginger and pepper (if using). Cook for 5 minutes until they are softened.

Add the chicken, then sprinkle in the cumin, ground coriander and turmeric and keep stirring over a fairly high heat, until their aroma is released.

Pour in the tomatoes and your sugar and stock. Bring up to the bubble and then simmer for 10 minutes until the chicken is cooked through. Stir in a pinch of garam masala.

Mix the cornflour with a couple of tablespoons of the hot stock from the pan, then return to the pan and stir until you have a rich and thickened sauce.

Serve, garnished with the yogurt, chopped fresh coriander and the optional dry-fried nigella seeds, with 5 tablespoons of basmati rice per person.

34 CALS / **0.8g** FAT / **0.5g** SAT FAT / **2.8g** SUGARS / **0.07g** SALT

CUCUMBER, ONION AND MINT RAITA

This raita goes beautifully with all the dishes in this section, especially if you add any extra chilli to them, as it does a wonderful job of taking the heat out of the situation! I sometimes have this with steamed vegetables and spicy rice when I fancy a meat-free day.

SERVES 4

300g cucumber, peeled and finely
  chopped
150ml low-fat Greek yogurt
1 teaspoon dried mint
¼ onion, peeled and grated
a small handful of fresh mint
salt

Place the cucumber in a sieve and sprinkle with salt . Leave it for about ten minutes until the excess juice runs out. Then stir into the yogurt along with the dried mint. Stir the onion into the mix and you're ready to go! Serve sprinkled with fresh mint.

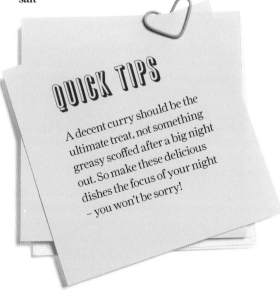

QUICK TIPS

A decent curry should be the ultimate treat, not something greasy scoffed after a big night out. So make these delicious dishes the focus of your night – you won't be sorry!

464 CALS / **19.1g** FAT / **10.4g** SAT FAT / **36.9g** SUGARS / **1.27g** SALT

SPINACH AND POTATO CURRY

It's easy to make the mistake of ordering a vegetable curry, thinking that it will be nice and healthy. You'd be right, in a way, as, if you take the meat out, you're going to take out a fair few calories, too. But what a lot of restaurants will then do is add a big spoonful of ghee to make up for the missing meat! Well, not in this recipe, which is rich in flavour from the spices and coconut milk. The carrot salad that is served alongside it makes it a real feast!

SERVES 4

1 tablespoon coconut/vegetable oil
2 medium onions, chopped
4 garlic cloves, quartered
2cm piece fresh ginger, grated
1 red chilli, finely chopped
2 heaped tablespoons Rogan Josh curry paste
3 medium potatoes, cut into 2cm chunks
1 small caulifower, cut into florets
8 medium ripe tomatoes, chopped
200g passata
400ml light coconut milk
500g washed babyleaf spinach
small bunch coriander, chopped

For the carrot salad
juice of 1 lemon
½ tablespoon sunflower oil
a good pinch of salt
8 large carrots, grated
1 tablespoon nigella seeds, or a couple of tablespoons finely chopped coriander

Heat the oil in a large, non-stick frying pan or wok. Cook the onions, garlic, ginger and chilli until softened. Add your curry paste. Carry on cooking, whilst stirring, until it looks nice and sticky and the aroma from the paste has been released. This should take a minute or two.

Now add your potatoes and cauliflower and stir in those yummy spices for a couple of minutes.

Next add the chopped tomatoes, passata and coconut milk. Bring back up to the bubble, then cover and simmer until the potato and cauliflower are cooked through.

Meanwhile, make the carrot salad. Mix together the lemon, oil and salt and pour over the grated carrots. If using nigella seeds, dry-fry in a very hot non-stick pan until they pop a little and then stir into the salad. If using coriander, just stir it in.

When the potatoes and cauliflower are cooked through, take the curry off the heat, stir in your spinach (we just want to wilt it so as to keep all the gorgeous green and vitamins in), sprinkle over the coriander, and serve with the carrot salad. If you like, you can also have a cup of cooked basmati rice.

305 CALS / **6g** FAT / **1.1g** SAT FAT / **3.1g** SUGARS / **0.72g** SALT

MEXICAN CHICKEN FAJITAS

Now I am probably a very bad influence, but I would recommend a nice cold beer with these spicy little darlings!

SERVES 4

3 skinless, boneless chicken
   breasts, finely sliced into strips
1 medium red onion, finely sliced
2 medium garlic cloves, grated
4 tortilla wraps

For the marinade
1 teaspoon dried oregano
1 tablespoon (or to taste) hot
   smoked paprika
juice of ½ lime
1 small chilli pepper, finely sliced
   (optional)
salt and freshly ground black
   pepper

Preheat the oven to 200°C/Gas 6.

Mix the chicken breasts, onion and garlic together with the marinade ingredients. Marinate for minutes or hours, depending on how long you have!

Wrap the tortillas in tinfoil and warm in the oven.

Heat a heavy frying pan to a very high heat and toss in the chicken, onion and garlic along with all the marinade ingredients. Keep mixing and frying until the chicken is cooked through, about 3 minutes – be careful not to overcook, as the chicken can dry out very suddenly.

Serve with the warmed tortillas or Spicy Mexican Rice (page 176) and Chunky Salsa (page 177).

45 **25** 15
MINUTES
0 30

212 CALS / **3g** FAT / **0.3g** SAT FAT / **6.7g** SUGARS / **1.42g** SALT

SPICY MEXICAN RICE

I often make double the amount of this delicious rice and then take it for my packed lunch. Feel free to mix and match the veg and, if you like it hot, why not add some extra chilli sauce?

SERVES 4

½ tablespoon sunflower oil
1 medium onion, chopped
1 garlic clove, finely chopped
1 jalapeño chilli, deseeded and
  chopped (optional)
½ tablespoon tomato purée
1 teaspoon ground cumin
150g basmati rice
150g tinned or frozen sweetcorn
1 medium tomato, cubed
1 chicken or veg stock cube
freshly chopped coriander, for a
  bit of a garnish flourish!

Heat the oil in a saucepan and fry the onion and garlic for 2–3 minutes, stirring all the time. Throw in the chopped chilli and stir for another 30 seconds. Now stir in the tomato purée and the cumin and fry for a few seconds.

Tip in the rice and stir until it's well coated with the other ingredients. Add the sweetcorn and cubed tomato and give it all a good stir.

Pour in enough boiling water to cover the rice by about 2cm and crumble in the stock cube. Bring to the bubble for 1 minute. Stir just once and then reduce the heat, cover and simmer over a very low heat for 15 minutes until small holes begin to appear in the top of the rice. Don't lift the lid before the 15 minutes is up. Serve garnished with chopped fresh coriander.

QUICK TIPS

You can increase the rice in this recipe if some of the diners aren't dieting, but make sure you stick to the correct portion!

94 CALS / **7g** FAT / **1.4g** SAT FAT / **5.1g** SUGARS / **0.03g** SALT

CHUNKY SALSA

Why buy a jar full of ready made salsa when this lovely fresh one is so much healthier – and so easy to make?

SERVES 4

1 avocado, cubed
4 medium tomatoes, cubed
1 red onion, finely chopped
2–3 tablespoons lime juice
1 teaspoon dried oregano
4 tablespoons finely chopped fresh
   coriander
salt

Put the avocado, tomatoes and onion in a pretty serving bowl. Season the lime juice to taste with salt, stir in the oregano and pour into the bowl. Toss well and stir in the chopped fresh coriander to serve.

This gorgeous salsa can also make a great accompaniment to the chips on page 147.

LAZY SUNDAYS

Something special for when you have a little more time to cook

CRAZY LAZY SUNDAY

So, after all the rules, regulations, suggestions, recommendations, stipulations, mustn't-do thises and must-do thats, having divulged all my pearls of wisdom regarding the ways in which we can lose weight and yet still eat tastily, I am now going to give you all a collective slap on the back – a great big culinary hug from one Greedy Girl to another. I'm going to get off my greedy soap box and actually say that just once in a while, you – yes, YOU – are allowed to spend a bit more time enjoying yourself in the kitchen!

This is the section that appeals to the indulgent home cook within all of us. The Greedy Girl who just loves that end of the week, warm and glowing feeling of kicking back, hiding all the clocks, ignoring all the demands of our loved ones, chucking on some classic tunes or simply turning on our favourite soaps and doing that thing that often gets forgotten when constantly taking calories into consideration: actually enjoying the process of cooking food. God forbid!

Being a Greedy Girl, always on the look out for rogue calories that need zapping or eliminating, it's easy to forget that the actual act of cooking is in and of itself something to be relished and enjoyed to the full.

Well – here you go. It's the Lazy Sundays section. A chance to slow down, take in a deep draught of air and breeeeeeeaaathe.

YES! It's Sunday! A day to relax and unwind – not the LAST day of the weekend, more the FIRST chance to slow down.

Sunday is my favourite day of the week; the chance to pop open a bottle and spend a bit more time in the kitchen, carefully cooking something gorgeous to share with friends and family.

Sunday is also a day (I will not lie!) to loosen the belt a wee bit (notice I only say 'wee bit') and enjoy a little more of everything the kitchen allows!

If everyone else is allowed to have a Lazy Sunday up to one's elbows in recipe books, pots, pans, casserole dishes and glasses of rosé, well, what's wrong with a diet book also proposing a very similar end to the week?!

Let's face it, any diet book (no matter

what else it promises) that tells you that you can't have an indulgent lazy Sunday, is probably going to end up unceremoniously dumped in the bin!

But don't get me wrong. This doesn't mean we should give ourselves over to wild face-stuffing madness, like the dreaded skinnies would! Neither should we surrender to the 'monster muncher', especially having successfully kept him at arm's length for the previous six days. No. This would be diet suicide. It would lead us towards the kind of carnage that doesn't bear thinking about; resulting in us all being guilt-ridden, gibbering (fat) wrecks!

We have to be far cleverer than that. We have to feel like we are having it all without actually having all the calories.

Impossible, you say? Not so!

I've done all the work for you by subtly shaving away the calories but none of the flavour. So over the next few pages there is an abundance of gorgeous recipes that will allow you to indulge not only your love of eating, but also your love of cooking, too.

They will take a little more time to prepare than any of the other recipes in

Sunday is my favourite day of the week; the chance to pop open a bottle and spend a bit more time in the kitchen, carefully cooking something gorgeous to share.

the book but, hey, that's what we want on a Sunday. A little like the phrase 'faking it to make it', a Greedy Girl's Lazy Sunday is ALL about getting the set dressing right: making sure the right soundtrack is on, ensuring that all the family extras are either out of the house or certainly out of the kitchen. It's all about surrounding yourself with the props and creating the ambience that goes with a fully calorie-laden Sunday blow out... without quite cooking up the calories to match! Coming your way are Sunday roasts with all the trimmings, some brilliantly smoky barbecue feasts, dreamy, creamy summer stews, magical meringues, light-as-air sponges... even champagne jellies, to name just a few.

477 CALS / **29g** FAT / **8.2g** SAT FAT / **4g** SUGARS / **0.43g** SALT

HERBY ROAST CHICKEN

Is there anything more soothing than the aroma of a chicken roasting in the oven? Yes... of course there is! Eating a chicken roasted in the oven!

SERVES 4

2 tablespoons olive oil

1.5–2kg plumptious organic chicken

1 tablespoon dried parsley

1 tablespoon dried sage

1 tablespoon dried rosemary

1 tablespoon dried thyme

2 sticks celery, chopped

6 garlic cloves, whole

1 small onion, cut into eighths

2 carrots, cut into chunks

a couple of glugs of white wine

salt and freshly ground black pepper

Preheat the oven to its highest setting.

Rub the oil all over the birdie's skin and season inside and out, then rub in half of the herbs.

Put the celery, garlic, onion, carrots and the rest of the herbs into a baking tray. Put the chicken on top, and place in the middle of the oven for 20 minutes.

Take the tray out, baste the bird with the juices, and lower the oven temperature to 180°C/Gas 4.

Pour the wine into the bottom of the pan, making sure you don't pour it over the chicken, and return to the oven. If you're making Roasties (page 185) too, now's the time to add them to the oven.

Roast the chicken for another 45 minutes, or until the juices run clear, then remove the chicken from the oven and keep warm while you whack up the temperature to finish off the Roasties.

Serve with the Roasties, Yorkshire Puddings and Parsley and Shallot Carrots (page 184), and your favourite green veg, plus, of course, lashings of low-fat gravy.

25 MINUTES

87 CALS / 2.67g FAT / 0.87g SAT FAT / 1.4g SUGARS / 0.1g SALT

YORKSHIRE PUDDINGS

For all you non-British Greedy Girls out there, we know how weird the whole idea of Yorkshire pudding is – but I urge you to try them, as they really satisfy 'the greedy need'!

MAKES 6

2 large eggs
80g plain flour
150ml milk
pinch of salt

Get the oven as hot as you can. Grease a six-hole silicone muffin tray. Put the eggs, flour, milk and salt into a bowl and whisk together.

Pour the batter into your silicone moulds and put in the oven for 20 minutes or until risen and golden brown.

10 MINUTES

111 CALS / 2g FAT / 0.3g SAT FAT / 19.3g SUGARS / 0.17g SALT

PARSLEY AND SHALLOT CARROTS

Simply adding a little parsley and sautéed shallot makes all the difference here.

SERVES 4

12 carrots, julienned
½ tablespoon olive oil
1 shallot, finely chopped
2 tablespoons chopped fresh
   flat-leaf parsley
pinch of sugar

Steam the carrots until tender – about 4 minutes, depending on their size. Meanwhile, heat the olive oil in a sauté pan over a medium heat and fry the shallots until softened. Stir in the parsley and steamed carrots and a wee pinch of sugar before serving.

224 CALS / **9g** FAT / **1g** SAT FAT / **1.2g** SUGARS / **0.03g** SALT

ROASTIES

Nobody wants boiled potatoes on a Sunday, do they ? No! Nobody wants steamed potatoes on a Sunday, do they? No! What do we want? We want roasties! We want roasties! The bigger the potatoes, the less fat they absorb, so you could, if you want, leave them whole – but they will take a little longer to cook.

SERVES 4

8 floury potatoes (Maris Piper,
   Desirée or King Edward), peeled
   and halved
3 tablespoons vegetable oil
sea salt flakes

Preheat the oven to 180°C/Gas 4.

Pop the potatoes into a saucepan of salty water and bring them to the boil, then simmer them until they are just tender. Drain. If you have time, let them cool.

Next, scratch the potatoes all over with a fork (this ensures that you get very crispy roasties, and is far more effective than just bashing them around in the pan, as some folks do).

Pour the oil into a baking tray, put it in the oven and let it heat up for 10 minutes. Then add your potatoes to the baking tray and toss them in the oil. It's important that the potatoes aren't too cosy in the pan, or they will steam rather than roast. So, if necessary, use two baking trays.

Roast in the oven for between 50 and 60 minutes, increasing the oven temperature to 210–220°C/Gas 7 for the last 15 minutes. I do quite a bit of turning and moving my potatoes around throughout the cooking time, so that every single one of them is totally crisp and golden all over. If you don't have time to do that, don't worry – they'll still be lovely – but it's that extra bit of TLC that takes these babies to another level!

Serve with the rest of your roast.

341 CALS / **10g** FAT / **3.2g** SAT FAT / **7.9g** SUGARS / **1.46g** SALT

SUPER SUMMER CHICKEN STEW

Can you imagine anything tasting better than garlicky, lemony, creamy chicken, finished off with olives and new potatoes, accompanied by a glass of crisp white wine, in the company of good friends, on a beautiful summer's day..? No, neither can I!

SERVES 4

1 tablespoon olive oil
1 red onion, sliced
4 garlic cloves, quartered
5 sprigs lemon thyme
6 chicken thighs, skin removed
300ml chicken stock
10 new potatoes, steamed until
   just tender
2 carrots, julienned
100g frozen petits pois
zest of 1 lemon
10 green olives
3 tablespoons low-fat cream
chopped fresh parsley or chives,
   to serve
salt and freshly ground black
   pepper

Heat the oil in a casserole dish and gently fry the onion until soft but not coloured. Add the garlic and cook until slightly softened.

Add the thyme and chicken and pour the chicken stock over the top (adding more if needed – it must cover the chicken). Season well and throw in the potatoes. Bring up to the bubble and then simmer for 15–25 minutes.

Then add the carrots, petits pois, lemon zest and olives and season. Cook until the chicken is cooked through. Stir in the cream, divide between four bowls and serve topped with the chopped parsley or chives.

294 CALS / **20g** FAT / **7.4g** SAT FAT / **3.9g** SUGARS / **1.49g** SALT

KORMA BALLS (NOT KARMA BALLS)

This is a great dish to make the day before if you are having people over for Sunday lunch, as it tastes even better the next day. You can, of course, add some chillies when you fry the onions if you fancy a bit of a kick in the face! If you're going to make it ahead of time, don't add the flaked almonds until just before you eat or they will go soggy, and make sure you serve it piping hot!

SERVES 4

400g British pork mince
1 teaspoon cumin
1 teaspoon dried coriander
4 tablespoons finely chopped fresh
   coriander or flat-leaf parsley
1 tablespoon oil
1 onion, finely chopped
2 garlic cloves, chopped
2 tablespoons Korma curry paste
175ml light coconut milk
500ml chicken stock
16 cherry tomatoes, halved
1 tablespoon flaked almonds
salt and freshly ground black
   pepper

To make the meatballs, put the mince, cumin, dried coriander and fresh coriander (or parsley) into a bowl with some salt and pepper and mix thoroughly. Then wet your hands (so the meat doesn't stick to them) and shape the meat into walnut-sized balls.

Heat a large, non-stick frying pan over a medium heat. Pour in the oil and fry the meatballs, in batches if necessary, turning the whole time until browned all over. Remove from the pan with a slotted spoon and set aside.

Reduce the heat to very low. Add the onion to the pan and fry gently until softened, then add the garlic and cook until softened. Now add the curry paste to the onion and garlic mixture and fry over a low heat.

Pour in the coconut milk and stock and bring it up to the bubble, then turn the heat down to low. Add the meatballs and cook gently for about 10 minutes until the pork is cooked through, but be careful not to overcook or the pork will become dry. Add the tomatoes and cook for a couple more minutes, then serve, scattered with the flaked almonds.

Serve with basmati rice.

336 CALS / **9g** FAT / **4.2g** SAT FAT / **17.1g** SUGARS / **0.53g** SALT

VEGETABLE LASAGNE

This fabulous lasagne takes a little more time than most of the dishes in this book, but it really is worth it – and so are you, so why not treat yourself?

SERVES 4

2 aubergines, sliced into 1cm-thick
   rounds
spray olive oil
2 teaspoons mixed spice
2 medium courgettes, cut in half
   and sliced length ways
2 red onions, sliced into rounds
2 garlic cloves, sliced
handful of cherry tomatoes
110g dried lasagne
handful of spinach leaves
125g ball low-fat mozzarella,
   grated, shredded or sliced
30g low-fat mature Cheddar
   cheese
salt and freshly ground black
   pepper

For the white sauce
500ml skimmed milk
½ onion, finely chopped
10 peppercorns
1 bay leaf
2–3 tablespoons cornflour
a grating of nutmeg
3 tablespoons freshly grated
   Parmesan cheese

You will need two baking trays and an ovenproof dish measuring 25 x 18cm. Preheat the oven to 200°C/Gas 6.

Lay the aubergines on a baking tray, spray with olive oil and sprinkle with salt and the mixed spice. Put the courgettes and red onions on another baking tray, spray with olive oil and sprinkle with salt and the sliced garlic. Pop both trays in the oven and bake for 30 minutes or until light golden brown.

Meanwhile, make the sauce. Pour the milk into a non-stick pan and add the onion, peppercorns and bay leaf. Let it simmer for a few minutes, then leave to infuse for 10 minutes off the heat. Put the cornflour in a small bowl and then stir in a couple of tablespoons of the warmed milk to make a paste. Now pour it back into the milk mixture and whisk, whilst simmering, for 5 minutes until the sauce is thickened. Add a grating of nutmeg and the Parmesan and season well.

When the aubergines, courgettes and red onions are beautifully roasted, remove from the oven (but leave the oven on). Put a layer of the roasted veg in the bottom of your ovenproof dish and then scatter half the cherry tomatoes on top and drizzle over a third of the white sauce. Then top with a layer of lasagne and repeat the process. Next sprinkle the spinach on top, then lay another layer of lasagne on top and pour over the rest of the sauce. Top with the mozzarella and the Cheddar.

Bake in the oven for 30 minutes or until the pasta is cooked through. Serve with a huge green salad.

0
45 **15** 15
MINUTES
30

48 CALS / **1g** FAT / **0.1g** SAT FAT / **6.2g** SUGARS / **0.01g** SALT

SMOKY AUBERGINES AND COURGETTES

Although these vegetables are lovely served hot, I always like to make extra, as they are delicious served in sandwiches the next day.

SERVES 10

5 medium aubergines, sliced
5 courgettes, sliced
spray olive oil
1 tablespoon cinnamon (optional)
seeds from 1 large pomegranate
handful of roughly chopped fresh
   flat-leaf parsley
salt and freshly ground black
   pepper

Spray the vegetables all over with the oil. Sprinkle with salt, pepper and cinnamon, if you're using it.

Now place the vegetables on the barbecue and cook until beautifully charred, smoky and softened. Transfer to a serving plate, sprinkle with the pomegranate seeds and parsley and make it all as pretty as a picture.

QUICK TIPS

Thirsty aubergines are notorious for guzzling up oil when you fry them, so spraying them with a little oil and then grilling them means you get all the taste and texture without the extra fat.

112 CALS / 2g FAT / 0.3g SAT FAT / 1.2g SUGARS / 0.64g SALT

RUSTIC TOMATO GARLIC BREAD

This is a great way to indulge in the joys of garlic bread and still hear the angels singing, as it is low fat but still delicious! Make sure you use a rough rustic bread so that you almost grate the garlic and tomato with it.

SERVES 10

2 large garlic cloves, peeled
10 slices of rustic bread
2 medium tomatoes
spray olive oil
sea salt

Cut the garlic cloves in half and rub them over the bread. Then cut the tomatoes in half and rub them over the bread. Now spray with olive oil, sprinkle with sea salt and grill on both sides on the barbie!

QUICK TIPS

This is definitely a great dish to serve as a side when you're cooking for large groups – it goes with almost anything, and can also make a lovely light lunch served with a big fresh salad.

148 CALS / **8g** FAT / **3.6g** SAT FAT / **0.2g** SUGARS / **0.14g** SALT

HERBY LAMB CHOPS

The yogurt in this marinade makes the lamb so tender and these chops go beautifully with the Smoky Aubergines and Courgettes (page 190). You can use exactly the same marinade for chicken, if you prefer.

SERVES 10

4 tablespoons Greek yogurt

2 garlic cloves, minced

2 tablespoons chopped fresh
  rosemary

2 tablespoons chopped fresh
  thyme

zest and juice of 1 lemon

10 lamb chops (trimmed of fat)

Mix together the yogurt, garlic, herbs and lemon juice and zest and pour over the lamb chops. Leave to marinate for at least an hour, but even better overnight.

Grill for 5–8 minutes under a hot grill or on a hot barbecue (but not before the coals are white and the flames have died down, or the meat will burn on the outside and be left raw in the middle!).

Serve with the Smoky Aubergines and Courgettes (page 190), Rustic Tomato Garlic Bread (page 193) and a large mixed salad.

30 MINUTES 0 15 30 45

157 CALS / **5g** FAT / **2.2g** SAT FAT / **18.5g** SUGARS / **0.11g** SALT

STRAWBERRY SWISS ROLL

Strawberries, cream, cake – what's not to love?

SERVES 8

low-fat spread, for greasing
3 eggs
115g caster sugar
75g plain flour, sifted
icing sugar, for dusting (optional)

For the filling
150ml low-fat cream
1 tablespoon icing sugar
1 teaspoon vanilla extract
150g strawberries, hulled
 and sliced

Preheat the oven to 200°C/Gas 6. Grease a 30 x 20cm Swiss Roll tin and line with non-stick baking paper.

Put the eggs and caster sugar in a bowl and whisk until thick and mousse-like and doubled in size – this will probably take about ten minutes, so if you have a stand alone mixer you are going to be as happy as Larry!

Fold in the sifted flour really carefully with a large metal spoon so as not to bang out any of the lovely air bubbles you have made! Then carefully pour in 1 tablespoon boiling water and stir in gently.

Spoon the batter into your tin and spread it evenly to the edges. Pop it into the oven and bake for about 10–12 minutes, or until the cake springs back when you press it lightly.

When your sponge is ready, spread a sheet of greaseproof paper out on a flat surface, sprinkle with the icing sugar (if using) and invert the cake on top. Peel the baking paper off the bottom and carefully roll the cake up. Leave it to cool.

Whisk the cream, icing sugar and vanilla extract together. Once the cake is cool, gently unroll it and spread it with the vanilla cream and strawberries. Now you just need to roll it up again and serve! Yum yum!

249 CALS / **3g** FAT / **0.6g** SAT FAT / **46.8g** SUGARS / **0.49** SALT

APPLE CHARLOTTE

This is my go-to dish whenever my mum comes over for lunch – which means I get to make it quite a lot, as she lives next door!

SERVES 4

2 tablespoons low-fat spread
50g fresh white breadcrumbs
50g soft light brown sugar, plus
   another tablespoon
4 tablespoons golden syrup
zest and juice of 2 lemons
800g cooking apples, peeled,
   cored and quartered, then cut
   into thin slices

Preheat the oven to 180°C/Gas 4. Grease and line a 1.7 litre pudding dish.

Melt the spread over a low heat in a small saucepan with the breadcrumbs. Sauté for a few minutes until the crumbs are golden and fairly crisp and then tip them out and leave them to cool slightly.

Heat the 50g sugar, syrup and lemon zest and juice gently in a small saucepan. Add the breadcrumbs and mix well.

Lay half of the apples in your dish and sprinkle with the remaining tablespoon of sugar. Top with a thin layer of the crumbs, then the rest of the apples and finish with the rest of the sweet crumbs.

Bake in the oven for 30 minutes until the crumbs are golden and the apples are soft.

Serve with low-fat cream or ice cream... just a little.

45 MINUTES

425 CALS / **17g** FAT / **6.6g** SAT FAT / **28.2g** SUGARS / **1g** SALT

PASTRY-WRAPPED APPLES

This is a really nifty way to have apple pie without consuming the thousands of calories you would with a traditional one – and the children just love that they get 'a whole pie' each!

SERVES 4

4 dessert apples
2 teaspoons ground cinnamon or ginger
75g raisins
375g light ready-rolled puff pastry
1 egg yolk, beaten
caster sugar, for sprinkling

Preheat oven to 220°C/Gas 7. Line a baking tray with baking paper.

Peel the apples and core them. Rub them inside and out with the cinnamon or ginger and then divide the raisins between them, putting them in the holes left by the cores.

Lightly flour a clean surface and roll out the pastry a little more, then cut it into four squares. Brush the edges with the egg yolk and then fold each square around an apple, cutting off any excess. Make the excess pastry into leaves and stick onto the top with egg yolk.

Sprinkle with a little caster sugar, place on the baking tray and bake until the pastry is nice and golden (about 40 minutes). Serve hot or cold with low-fat custard or ice cream.

When I make this for my husband, I swap the raisins for dates – try it!

541 CALS / **38g** FAT / **21.3g** SAT FAT / **31.5g** SUGARS / **1.05g** SALT

RASPBERRY CHEESECAKE

Right, this recipe definitely involves a bit of faffing about, but come on, my little greedies – we're talking cheesecake!!!

SERVES 6

75g reduced-fat butter
150g light digestive biscuits, crumbled
300g low-fat cream cheese
125g caster sugar
1 teaspoon vanilla extract
3 gelatine leaves
150ml low-fat double cream
300g raspberries
1 large egg white

To serve
handful of raspberries
handful of blueberries

Melt the butter in a saucepan over a low heat. Add the biscuits and stir really well.

Press the crumb mixture into a 18cm loose-bottomed tin using the flat of your hand or the back of a spoon. Put it in the fridge for about 20–30 minutes until it's thoroughly chilled.

Now put the cream cheese, sugar and vanilla extract into a bowl and beat well. Put the gelatine leaves into a bowl of cold water and let them soften.

Pour half the cream into a saucepan over a medium heat. Bring it just up to the bubble and then take it off the heat. Now squeeze the water from the gelatine and add the softened leaves to your hot cream. Stir it until the gelatine dissolves (ahhhh, cooks' pleasures).

Put the raspberries into a bowl and crush them up a bit. Add the cream-and-gelatine mix to the cream-cheese-and-sugar mix (did you get that, not sure if I did!), whilst beating it well, and pour in the rest of the cream. Now stir in the crushed raspberries.

Pour your egg white into a scrupulously clean (if there's any trace of grease, this won't work) bowl and whisk it until you get stiff peaks before gently folding it into the cream cheese mixture. Pour this gorgeousness over your chilled biscuit base and put in the fridge overnight.

Serve topped with the extra raspberries and blueberries.

45 | 0 | 15 | 1 HOUR | 30

184 CALS / **1g** FAT / **0.4g** SAT FAT / **41.6g** SUGARS / **0.15g** SALT

RASPBERRY PAVLOVA

My five-year-old calls this rather heavenly and sophisticated raspberry and cream meringue 'boomerang pie' and so, for me, that's what it shall be called for time immemorial.

SERVES 6

3 egg whites
200g caster sugar
1 teaspoon cornflour
2 teaspoons raspberry vinegar
1 teaspoon vanilla extract
350g raspberries

For the vanilla cream
200ml low-fat double cream or
   Greek yogurt
1 tablespoon icing sugar, plus
   more to serve (optional)
1 teaspoon vanilla extract

Preheat the oven to 160°C/ Gas 3. Line a baking tray with baking paper.

Using an electric whisk, beat the egg whites until they form peaks. Add the sugar a tablespoon at a time, continuing to whisk, and then whisk in the cornflour, vinegar and vanilla extract. Keep whisking until the mixture is smooth, glossy and forms stiff peaks.

Now spoon the meringue mixture on to the prepared tray and make a hollow in the middle to hold the lovely vanilla cream! Bake for 45 minutes and then leave to cool in the oven with the door ajar.

To make the vanilla cream, whisk the cream or Greek yogurt, icing sugar and vanilla extract together until thickened. Spoon into the pavlova and top with the raspberries. If you like, you can finish it off with a sprinkling of icing sugar.

Make sure your eggs are at room temperature before you start to get the best meringue.

25 MINUTES PLUS CHILLING

101 CALS / 0g FAT / 0g SAT FAT / 11.3g SUGARS / 0.05g SALT

CHAMPAGNE AND PEACH JELLIES

There isn't actually any need to use Champagne here – in fact, my mother would describe it as sacrilege – but I love the decadence of it all!

SERVES 4

350ml sugar-free lemonade
11g sachet of gelatine
2 tablespoons icing sugar
juice of ½ lemon
250ml Champagne or sparkling
 white wine
2 peaches or nectarines, stoned
 and sliced

Pour the lemonade into a small pan over a medium heat and bring it up to the bubble. Take the pan off the heat and sprinkle in the gelatine and sugar. Whisk until it's all dissolved and leave to cool.

Once cool, add the lemon juice and Champagne. Divide the peach slices equally between four glasses and then pour the jelly mix on top. Put in the fridge and leave to chill and set for 5 hours or overnight.

QUICK TIPS

You can swap the peaches here for any fruit you fancy, from plums to raspberries and strawberries – so experiment!

LET'S GET PHYSICAL

No book with 'diet' in the title should be without an all-singing, all-dancing section on the power of exercise... STOP!

Please don't groan and turn the page in a frantic bid to hunt out which pages the desserts are on! (I know you so well!) That's exactly what I would have done. Yup, for decades I sat on my fat arse laughing at 'all the nutters who exercised'. I vividly remember sitting in the car with my husband and with pure unadulterated envy I would laugh at and mock all the passing runners! We would describe them as smug, self-obsessed health loons who needed to get out (to the pub) more and enjoy the finer things in life – like food, drink and passing out!!! The fact that all these 'nutters' were, of course, slim, with great skin and enormous smiles on their faces, oh yes, and buttocks that didn't hit the floor each time their foot hit the pavement; all of these positive things, I simply chose to ignore! Instead, I would marvel at why on earth they were bothering to get sweaty when they surely must surely have had a sofa somewhere they could have been lying on instead!

I did, thank god, finally come to my senses in my forties (if only it had been my twenties!!) and eventually realised that, in fact, I was the sad self-obsessed nutter for NOT exercising! A nutter because, whether I liked it or not, it is a proven fact that, if we exercise, we live longer... in a slimmer body! Also, I just couldn't get my head round the fact that you can lead a healthier, more exercise-driven lifestyle AND indulge every now and then if you fancy it. Duh... what's not to like about that?!

But don't get me wrong – it can't be any old exercise. It's really important that you choose to do things you love when you exercise, otherwise – FACT – you WILL give up. You know it... I know it... An enormous industry is built around the inevitability of this fact!

But Girls, the really good news is that the gym is NOT the only option! If you love to boogie, well then turn up the music and boogie that butt off! If it's swimming that floats your boat, just swim it off instead. If running's your thing, then run like the wind and burn those calories like a good 'un! There are so many different ways to shift lard, get fit and stay fit without ever going anywhere near the dreaded gym. Mind you, though, if you love the gym, what are you waiting for? Get your kit on! But I know an awful lot of people who feel full of fear or mortal panic at the thought of going to the gym, or for whom it is simply too difficult to fit into a busy schedule; and, believe me, there is no failure like the feeling you've failed to do your gym workout. Indeed, it's often an invitation to stuff your face with chocolate eclairs!

But if none of the above gym-speak appeals to you I may have the perfect way for you to exercise – something you could only ever have dreamed of, something that certainly sounds too good to be true...

Its called The Lazy Workout (are you loving it already?) and it was created by my dear friend Jane Wake, a personal trainer and all-round top bird, who understands that an awful lot of us girls are highly unlikely to ever give over precious hours to work out their bodies! A busy working mum herself, she knows only too well how hard it is to fit in training alongside our careers, not to mention nappy changing, husband feeding, dishwasher stacking, supermarket shopping, dusting (personally I never dust!) hoovering, scrubbing, washing, etc, etc...

So rather fantastically, the Lazy Workout simply and cleverly incorporates daily exercise routines into your working day! So, whether you are doing the shopping, catching a bus, jumping on the Tube, working at your desk, or looking after the kids, you can exercise at the same time and not necessarily alter the course of your day! If the very idea of this concept makes you go YAHOO! with joy... Well, that's convenient, because Jane has developed The Lazy Workout into an online TV

It's a proven fact that, if we exercise, we live longer... in a slimmer body. You can lead a healthier, more exercise-driven lifestyle AND indulge every now and then if you fancy it. What's not to like about that?

series courtesy of Yahoo TV and you will hear my dulcet tones on the voiceover, too!! So, go on, open your laptop, and go to http://uk.lifestyle.yahoo.com/diet-fitness/lazy-workout. Within 10 minutes, you'll have probably burnt some calories!!! Any workout plan that suggests exercises for when you're standing at the bar with a cocktail in your hand gets my vote of approval!

INDEX

INDEX

I would like to thank...

All the girls out there who made the first *Greedy Girl's Diet* such a success so that we could all have second helpings!!

My beloved husband and our four beautiful girls for all the joy they bring to my life.

My mad genius agent Neil Howarth for all his hard work, dedication and unfailing loyalty.

My dear friend Jane Wake for the brilliant Lazy Workout!

My publishers, Kyle Books.